DATE DUE

12·6·11			

Demco

SMART GREEN

———————

SMART GREEN
How to Implement Sustainable Business Practices in Any Industry and Make Money

---

Jonathan Estes

WILEY

John Wiley & Sons, Inc.

Published by John Wiley & Sons, Inc., Hoboken, New Jersey
Published simultaneously in Canada

For general information on our other products and services or for technical support, please contact our Customer Care Department within the United States at (800) 762-2974, outside the United States at (317) 572-3993 or fax (317) 572-4002.

Wiley also publishes its books in a variety of electronic formats. Some content that appears in print may not be available in electronic books. For more information about Wiley products, visit our web site at www.wiley.com.

Library of Congress Cataloging-in-Publication Data:

Estes, Jonathan.
Smart green : how to implement sustainable business practices in any industry and make money / by Jonathan Estes.
   p. cm.
   Includes Index.
   ISBN 978-0-470-38779-5 (cloth)
      1. Business enterprises—Environmental aspects.   2. Management—Environmental aspects.   3. Green products.   4. Sustainable development.   I. Title.
HD30.255.E84   2009
658.4'083—dc22

2008042915

Printed in the United States of America

10 9 8 7 6 5 4 3 2 1

I'd like to dedicate this book to my father, Ray Estes,
who has always believed in me from the beginning.

Contents

Acknowledgments   ix

Introduction   xi

Chapter 1   The Green Rush   1

Chapter 2   Taking the First Step—Becoming Aware   19

Chapter 3   Defining a Smart Green Company   41

Chapter 4   Smart Green Strategic Planning   67

Chapter 5   Measuring Sustainability Outcomes   93

Chapter 6   Marketing Green   113

Chapter 7   Building Smart Green Companies   131

Chapter 8   Smart Green Leadership   151

Appendix   179

Notes   189

Index   193

Acknowledgments

Encouragement for writing *Smart Green* came from a former editor of John Wiley & Sons, Inc., Don Odom, whose promised copy will be sent because of his enthusiasm for the subject of sustainability and his belief in me to write a compelling book proposal. There have been many others as well who have provided support, inspiration, and belief throughout the writing process, especially my wife, Jaleh; my two sons, Jordan and Gabe; and my stepdaughters, Nadia and Tahirih. I'd like to thank my parents, Ray and Joanne Estes, for having coffee ready every morning and for the great dialogues on themes I was exploring.

A special thanks goes to Miles Lane: I'm glad you suggested I pay attention to the topic of sustainability many years ago; I didn't listen, but I'm listening now. I'd like to thank my business partner, Zemo Trevathan, who challenged my thinking and my motives, and helped keep the message authentic. Rita Leadem, my assistant throughout the research and writing process, has been a tremendous help and an insightful reviewer. Thanks to Gart Davis, who came up with the concept of levels of "greenth" and inspired me to expand on the idea further.

I'd like to thank Aaron Nelson and the entire staff of the Chapel Hill Chamber of Commerce, who inspire us to realize that every individual and organization can make a difference, and can succeed financially while implementing a sustainability strategy. I'd like to extend special thanks to all of the business owners, managers, and other leaders who are in the trenches bravely trying to make a difference not only for their bottom lines, but for their communities and for the environment. To all of my reviewers—Rita Leadem, Barrie Trinkle, Frank Phoenix, Mike Knupp, and Aaron Nelson— thank you for helping me with accuracy, for stretching my ideas, and for keeping me honest.

Introduction

The world hates change, yet it is the only thing
that has brought progress.
                                        —*Charles Kettering*

Most likely you picked up this book because you're interested in going green but you're not clear about how to make the necessary changes without appearing like you're greenwashing—looking green without really being green—and continue to generate a profit. Perhaps you are seeking that tipping point of understanding and commitment toward a more sustainable enterprise or you are interested in launching a new company based on sustainable principles. As a consumer or investor, you may want to understand the criteria for what kinds of companies you would want to buy from, use as vendors for purchasing products and services, or invest in that share your values. Whatever your reason, I hope these pages add to your exploration and perhaps to your own tipping point.

In spite of global economic crises, for entrepreneurs eyeing the shift in consumer interest in all things green and sustainable, the game is afoot. At the height of the dot-com era, in major cities throughout the United States, there was a monthly event, known as a shooting gallery, specially planned for entrepreneurs to pitch their ideas to venture capital firms. I'll never forget the feeling I had when the names of entrepreneurs were called out like on *The Price Is Right*: "John Smith, come on down!" Wishing it were me, I watched John (not his real name) raise his hand amidst the throng of nearly 100 entrepreneurs, suited up with executive summaries in hand, who had come to acquire $1 million in venture capital from one of four venture capital firms. Another lucky entrepreneur's business card was drawn from a hat, and she gave a yelp and ran down to the front of the stage. Though I was hoping they would call me up in the next round, I also knew what it meant to be picked. Business owners had just three minutes to explain their product, their market, how they were going to reach that market and grow, and how much they needed and why. After that, if they were lucky, the venture partners would grill them with questions like "How do you plan to beat your competition?" "What is your exit strategy?"

and "Why should I care?" If they ran over the allotted time without finishing their presentation, too bad. Like being "gonged" on *The Gong Show*, they were pulled off the stage as another pair of hopeful entrepreneurs was called down.

Shooting galleries like this played out all over the country during the late 1990s, when everyone seemed to have a great idea to launch on the Web, including me. I mention this experience because that exciting upsurge of entrepreneurial energy and hope is back, now with even greater force and urgency than in the heyday of those early dot-coms. I'm speaking of the green or sustainability revolution that is already gaining momentum on a global scale—promoting the ideals of the so-called triple bottom line of social equity, environmental stewardship, and profits. This time, however, there is a mission behind the business madness: saving the planet from the effects of global warming and greater demand on diminishing resources. Add to that dreams of sustainable models that include redistribution of wealth, empowering local economies, and inspiring social equity, and we have a new, bona fide social movement.

One thing I've learned as a veteran of entrepreneurship: Business is tough, requiring unwavering commitment and timely intelligence to be successful. Most who attempt it lose. And no matter what your beliefs are and what you hope will happen, the basic principles of what make a business work remain the same. You still have to present your business plan including a stellar management team, an innovative product, a receptive market, competition to outmaneuver, and an exit strategy. You still have to face the periodic, persistent questions from your investors or stakeholders about your value. You have to be *smart* in a variety of ways, and *Smart Green* will guide you through some of the key issues and opportunities in the emerging world of sustainability, helping you avoid the pitfalls of what I term being perceived as "greenwashing"—adopting the outward aspects of sustainability for marketing and image purposes only.

The success of sustainability and the prosperity of everyone on our planet are in the hands of innovative entrepreneurs. At the Greenbuild Conference 2007 in Chicago, Illinois, where participation had jumped 70 percent over the previous year, former President Bill Clinton expressed the spirit of times: "We've got to prove, not only to ourselves but to the entire world, that this is not only something we have to do to save the planet for our children and grandchildren, but it is a *staggering* economic opportunity."

We are at a critical crossroads: Innovate or face the consequences of not having enough energy or resources to accommodate the growing demand. No one can shop, eat out, turn on the TV, listen to the radio, or log on to the Internet and not see or hear about green innovations, the perils of global warming, peak oil, rising fuel costs, and the melting polar ice caps. Meanwhile, we also see and hear an increase in the responses from businesses with new products, new marketing messages, and statements about how we as consumers need to think and act green.

Within the past couple of years, the awareness of green issues has reached a tipping point. Many doubters still believe it to be a trend that will rise and fall in cycles once the price of gasoline returns to normal, but an increasing number of consumers and businesses seem to agree that what we are experiencing is a revolution of green awareness and change. I believe that the conjoining of the entrepreneurial spirit and the ideals of sustainability—the reason I am writing this book—will demonstrate that not only are there tremendous business opportunities for sustainable enterprises, but the best hope for the world is actually in the hands of innovative entrepreneurs! What I also hope and expect you will gain from this book is the same thing I have always believed: that even in a time of crisis, your cup is half full and not half empty. Beyond this cliché, what I mean to convey is the thrill of living at the edge of your life in the pursuit of your dreams—building a successful business while making a meaningful difference in the world, even against seemingly impossible odds.

There is no greater force for change than that of the dreams of the entrepreneur, who, faced with doubt, adversity, and the ups and downs of success, perseveres to realize those dreams. In the summer of 2007 I was in a cybercafe in downtown Kampala during rolling brownouts (due to the reduction of hydroelectric power from Lake Victoria), and I spoke with enthusiastic young people who were starting laptop and cell phone businesses and making deals with the enthusiasm of the entrepreneurial spirit. I saw the same phenomenon in other places I traveled to, such as Delhi, India, and

Johannesburg, South Africa, and every day at Cup-a-Joe's Coffee Shop in my home base of Chapel Hill, North Carolina.

While there is an increasing interest in sustainability in the business community, there are few resources available that provide a practical guide and examples of sustainability and business success—a desirable resource among business owners who require less theory and more action.

In *Smart Green* I will share ideas from my own experiences and those of other business owners and managers, colleagues in the sustainability field, and those whose shoulders we've stood on throughout the years since long before sustainability was the watchword. I have spoken with many business owners about their green strategies, and I've been amazed at the creativity and innovation these business leaders shared with me; but most importantly, I was encouraged by the commitment and caring that I believe will carry them forward through the tough times. Chapters in the book expand on these concepts; provide a practical approach for you to begin thinking about sustainability and implementing meaningful and profitable outcomes; and, I hope, to inspire new businesses, connections to clients and partners, and innovations that build wealth and are good for the planet at the same time.

> **Big Idea 1:** There is a veritable Green Rush toward innovation and wealth building to which all organizations must adapt or possibly perish.

With the combination of growing global concern for the environment, increasing energy costs, and more informed consumers, entrepreneurs and investors are naturally attracted to the new opportunities enabled by the emerging green movement. There are still many significant gaps in products and services in every industry, generating a vacuum of supply when there are buyers with checks in hand. Meanwhile, entrepreneurs are realizing that these gaps cannot be filled with a simple redesign of their products or even new products without considering each component of sustainability—profitability, social equity, and environmental impact.

Big Idea 2: Entrepreneurs play a crucial role for innovation and success of sustainable solutions.

Some advantages entrepreneurs contribute to sustainable solutions include (1) willingness to take risks, (2) adaptability to adverse conditions, and (3) focus on cost-effective outcomes with an emphasis on return on investment. Traditionally viewed as the source of negative environmental impacts and insensitivity to social equity issues, entrepreneurs prove the contrary in most cases. In fact, entrepreneurs, representing many small business owners, have contributed a tremendous amount to advances in product design, production efficiencies, and effective distribution we enjoy while also inspiring significant increases in job growth, wages, and economic opportunity.

Big Idea 3: Measurement of business outcomes must demonstrate both cost savings and return on investment for long-term stakeholder support.

Proving financial value and profitability beyond cost savings and improving efficiency are fast becoming key performance indicators; however, business impact in the form of return on investment is not often measured for lack of an adequate mind-set for the changes required and a suitable measurement tool set. With the increasing changes in the global marketplace toward more environmentally sustainable models for products, entrepreneurs are eyeing the opportunities for new products or redevelopment of existing products to meet this new demand for green products and sustainable practices. Many business owners interested in a sustainable product model are seeking proof of profits, not just cost savings to mitigate their risk.

Big Idea 4: Sustainability is an integral, multifaceted system including product life cycle, business relationships, and business value.

For Smart Green companies to thrive they must see their impact from a systems-view perspective inclucive of three basic aspects: (1) A product life-cycle which determines the current impact your business is having from the point of extraction of resources to manufacture, to distribution, retail, and waste. (2) Current business relationships, which determine the impact your business is having upon each of the contributors and recipients of your products to encourage positive change in the circle of your company's sustainability impact. (3) Finally, demonstrating value with a business case inclusive of the environment, the community, and profits is vital before embarking on a sustainability strategy.

Beyond these Big Ideas, in this book I share with you the excitement, successes, and challenges of entrepreneurs and managers throughout the country and across many sectors. Their stories will sound familiar to those of you who have ever tried to take the risks associated with starting a new company or taking on a project requiring courage and creativity with skeptical stakeholders. Moreover, throughout the book, you'll have a chance to explore these Big Ideas in more detail and begin to answer some of the questions many entrepreneurs and managers have been asking:

- What is sustainability, and why should I care?

- What steps do I need to take to implement an effective sustainability strategic plan?

- How do I measure the impact of our sustainability initiatives in a way that demonstrates business impact and not just cost savings?

- What are the benefits and risks involved with marketing green initiatives?

- Should I invest in reducing environmental impact or in complete product and facility redesign?

- What will be the role of entrepreneurs in the sustainability revolution?

- What are the key issues entrepreneurs will have to overcome to be truly sustainable?

- Why is there a persistent tension between businesses and environmental and social activism? How can this tension be overcome?

Smart Green is not just for the emerging business owner or the visionary business manager. I consider all of us—consumers, public servants, nonprofit leaders, students, faculty, and anyone else who believes change needs to happen and who takes even the smallest step toward rethinking and innovating to make this world a better place for future generations—as true entrepreneurs. It's a risk worth taking, so let's roll up our sleeves, pull out the idea napkins, and innovate!

1

The Green Rush

In the middle of difficulty lies opportunity.

—*Albert Einstein*

THE TIMES THEY ARE A-CHANGIN'

You can't turn on the TV, read a newspaper, listen to the radio, or surf the Web without hearing about "going green," "climate change," and "sustainability." Obviously, the largest market crash since the Great Depression and fluctuating gasoline prices up to $4 per gallon helps to motivate people to conserve and consider alternative energy sources; but even before recent increases in the price of gas, consumers have been bombarded with a plethora of new advertising messages and images that assume we are concerned about toxins in our homes, organic and fair-trade ingredients in our food, and energy-efficient cars and appliances. I was struck by one Web site from a major facilities management firm that changed overnight from images of soaring skyscrapers and monstrous machinery to green fields and children playing in flower gardens. Why this sudden interest in going green among consumers and at every level of our corporate society? Is going green a real economic revolution, or is this yet another trendy topic that will burn out—until the next oil-dependency crisis? The winds of change are palpable not just by a few college students, environmental activists, political strategists, and consumer advocates; rather, the interest in green products and a sustainable lifestyle is becoming a major trend in the mainstream. For entrepreneurs, investors, corporate managers across all industries, there is a rush to become aware of all things green and to meet the new, emerging consumer demand. And behind this surge of interest to meet a market potential, there is a glimmer of interest in making a difference in the world: building a better community, making our environment a better place for all its inhabitants, and growing successful businesses.

THE TIPPING POINT

During the past several years, like most people, I had noticed an increase in the debate about whether global warming was caused by humans or a natural, temporary phenomenon. Most of the information I was hearing remained in the background as white noise, drowned out by the news of the day and my own concerns. I read about greenhouse gases, the ozone layer depletion, polar bears trapped on melting ice flows, peak oil, increasing droughts worldwide, and more catastrophic storms. Every once in a while, the news about climate change would impact me directly: It has been getting increasingly unbearably hot in North Carolina in the summer (topping 100 degrees and 90 percent humidity for days on end). But like many people, I was too busy running my company, paying the bills, raising a family, and being a consumer to care about changing global conditions. So I turned up the air-conditioning.

Meanwhile, a quiet revolution was taking place and a new vocabulary was emerging without me being completely aware of the implications. Terms like *sustainability, fair-trade, locally grown, shade-grown, no GMO* (genetically modified organism), *rainforest-friendly, toxin-free*, and *organic* began appearing on products, not just in the local health food cooperatives but in mainstream grocery stores. Concern for the environment, which has been around for decades, was beginning to become commercially significant. After starting with a trickle, suddenly the floodgates seemed to be flung open with the change of language, introduction of new products, and images of age-old companies rebranding themselves as green. A real shocker that made me look was when Clorox bought Burt's Bees and released a green cleaning product line!

The tipping point for me to begin looking at sustainability as a focus for my personal life and business took place in the fall of 2007 as a result of small pieces of information coming together at the right time. This is how change actually happens: I had just completed a three-year contract with a firm providing software for physicians treating patients with HIV/AIDS in the developing world, so I was already connecting the dots of how and where things are made, the widening gap between the haves and have-nots, and the depletion of natural resources abroad. Like many people, I was deeply moved by Al Gore's movie, *An Inconvenient Truth*[1] and inspired to start looking at ways I could change some of my own practices. I viewed a short documentary called "The Next Industrial Revolution: William McDonough,

Michael Braungart and the Birth of the Sustainable Economy"[2] about the financial benefits of redesigning products to be of high quality and not harmful to the environment from the time they are made to their disposal. Companies profiled in the McDonough/Braungart film demonstrated how it was possible to change the entire design of their product, be environmentally friendly, and make a profit.

As a business value analyst for the facilities management sector, I had observed many times how green initiatives such as changes to building design and reduction of energy costs benefited the organizations financially. For me, it wasn't just the cost savings in the short term—it was the long-term, measurable benefits of improved employee morale, which translate into better retention, less sick leave, and increased productivity. The myth about going green being too expensive began eroding with evidence of a meaningful return on investment (ROI). Also, at many facilities conferences I attended, an increasing number of facilities and production managers were coming with checks in hand to buy green products. (Even with the increased number of companies supplying green products today, a gap still remains between demand and the availability of a diversity of products that customers want.) The final contribution to my tipping point came from the book *Good News for a Change*.[3] I read about how businesses were changing and becoming concerned about the environment while still being financially successful, but equally important to me was the depth of change among the business owners, their employees, their customers, and their vendors. Against many obstacles, these businesses persevered in the belief that there must be a balance between being financially successful, a good steward of the environment, and committed to principles of social equity.

This interest in sustainability and all things green is actually a revolution in the same sense as the industrial revolution—a fundamental shift of our values and practices concerning financial means, how we interact with the environment, and how we treat each other. I was hooked. My background in international development, value analytics, and entrepreneurship found a home, and I'm now committed to inspiring others to find their own tipping points. The question is, will anything we do make a difference. Can the business community be an integral part of turning the tide of global public action to reverse many of the policies and practices in motion potentially accelerating rapid climate change? Many of the recent reports indicate there is a chance to avert significant disaster, but we have to act fast.

CLIMATE CHANGE: "THE GREATEST MARKET FAILURE THE WORLD HAS EVER SEEN"

The time is over keeping our heads in the sand about climate change and the effects of global warming. In the United Nations Intergovernmental Panel on Climate Change (IPCC) Fourth Assessment Report, "Climate Change 2007"[4] recommends immediate steps for stemming the tide of effects of global warming. The report asserts (supported by extensive peer review), "There is very high confidence that the net effect of human activities since 1750 has been one of warming." Their findings included the following:

Earth's surface temperature has increased 1.33 degrees Fahrenheit since 1900 (0.74 degrees Celsius), mostly in the past 50 years, likely making this the warmest period of the past 1,300 years. Eleven of the past 12 years have been the warmest years in the instrumental record, dating back to 1850.

Recent temperature and carbon dioxide (CO_2) emission trends are at the high end of the range forecast by the IPCC, with the global average temperature now rising about one-half degree Fahrenheit per decade. The frequency of heat waves, forest fires, and heavy-precipitation events has increased globally since 1950.

Areas affected by drought have spread globally since the 1970s. The incidence of coastal flooding has increased since 1975. Arctic sea ice cover has shrunk 20 percent since 1978, when satellite measurements began.

The rate of sea level rise has jumped 70 percent since 1993, compared to the prior 30-year measurement period. Rapid melting of the Greenland ice sheet is now raising new concerns that the amount of sea level rise that might occur this century will be measured in meters, not inches.

As startling and disconcerting as these statistics are, the most significant information from the report is the connection between these changes and that of human and financial losses increasing every day, and yet to come. From the rise of infectious diseases, loss of water sources, temperatures rising by 10 degrees Fahrenheit, sea level rising by two feet, worsening storms, and if CO_2 emissions are left unabated, "climate change could cause a 5 to 20 percent reduction in the projected global gross domestic product by 2050.5," according to *The Stern Review*. The former chief World Bank economist Sir Nicholas Stern called climate change "the greatest market failure the world has ever seen."[5] Add to this the global financial crisis and now more than ever there is a need for a shared collective vision for a new type of economics based on honesty, integrity, caring, and respect for each other, the planet, and our economic way of life.

WHAT IS SUSTAINABILITY AND WHY SHOULD I CARE?

Shortly after my own tipping point for taking sustainability more seriously, it was as if a light was turned on throughout the country. No matter where I turned, green was in. I was able to buy cloth bags for groceries at Target, I found an entire cable channel called Planet Green dedicated exclusively to green topics, and I just bought an organic cotton fair-trade T-shirt made in Nicaragua from Wal-Mart! It was like buying a new car, having never noticed the model before, and suddenly seeing everyone driving the same one. But I think it's more than that, because most of the people I spoke with all over the country were experiencing something similar: Climate change is real, whether or not humanity caused it; the human race has to change its behavior of unharnessed growth immediately or the planet and its inhabitants will suffer; and our current sources of energy, food production, and raw materials are being more rapidly depleted than previously predicted as emerging countries strive for the Western lifestyle. An old term has been resurrected to give a new meaning to the rising interest in green: Sustainability.

According to Andres Edwards in *The Sustainability Revolution*, sustainability can be summarized from the 1987 Brundtland Report as "development that meets the needs of the present without compromising the ability of future generations to meet their own needs," a definition that has evolved since then from discussions among business leaders, policy makers, and environmentalists from around the world.[6] The concept of sustainability has also been inclusive of conservation, the three Rs of reduce, recycle, reuse; and energy efficiency. From small, sustainable agricultural projects in the developing world to global conferences discussing economic implications of climate change, the concept of sustainability has been transformed to encompass three basic components, otherwise known as the triple bottom line (a term coined by John Elkington in his book *Cannibals with Forks: The Triple Bottom Line of 21st Century Business*),[7] which are inextricably linked to one another: people—the social equity aspect that implies ensuring the benefits of opportunity and equality for every human being; planet—the environmental aspect that implies preserving the natural qualities of our ecosystem for the benefit and health of future generations; and profits—the economic aspect that implies balancing financial growth with awareness and concern for the social good and environmental stewardship (see Figure 1.1).

As an entrepreneur, I noticed something different about the concept of sustainability: It unites normally contentious concepts such as social good and environmental stewardship with the goal of financial gain. If you are part of the business community or the environmental activist community, then you probably share my surprise at the implications of the widespread interest in this unity. Sustainability and the definition of the triple bottom line continue to evolve, being driven by a myriad of individuals, organizations, corporations, and government agencies worldwide toward an essentially common goal of reordering our existence as inhabitants of a planet with limited resources, a planet that is sensitive to our exertions of unbridled growth. No one group or interest owns the definition of sustainability or its application; however, an unprecedented number of individuals and organizations are adopting the basic principles and sharing results with others, inspiring a surge in innovation and new opportunities unparalleled in recent history—a sustainability revolution. Also, though the term "green" is interchangeable at times with "sustainable," there is a distinct difference. "Green" implies specific activities related to environmental impact whereas "sustainable" implies the inclusion of three activities that impact people, planet, and profits.

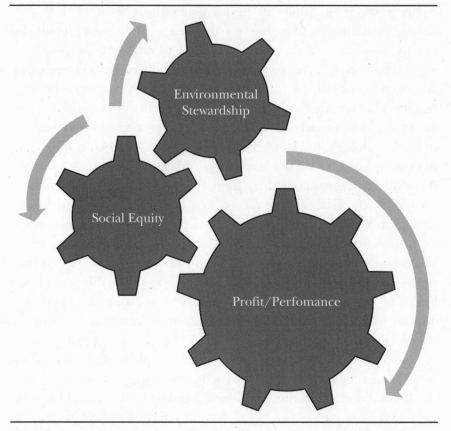

Figure 1.1   The Triple Bottom-line of Sustainability is comprised of interdependent outcomes including Environmental Stewardship, Social Equity, and Profit/Performance.

Meanwhile, a myth continues to persist that needs to dispelled: that individuals and small enterprises make little or no difference in the face of global climatic and social problems. In truth, every action we take as individuals, organizations, and societies has huge ramifications for the rest of the world. For now, keep in mind that our thoughts, decisions, and actions, which include purchasing, consuming, building, expanding, and growing in our home and community, have reverberating effects on other individuals, organizations, and societies that we can change with one informed decision. Make no mistake—sustainability is here to stay; and as Danny Ocean stated emphatically to his potential partners in the film *Ocean's Eleven*: "You're either in or you're out. Right now."

A PERFECT STORM

Actually, from an environmentalist perspective, the conditions for change toward a more sustainable society have never been more fertile. At the time of the writing of this book, the global economy was experiencing the greatest drop in value since the Great Depression, President elect Barack Obama promised unprecedented sustainability initiatives, and fuel prices were wildly fluctuating as the U.S. automakers were contemplating bankruptcy or bailout from the government. There has been a vacuum of accurate climate change data, while denials of the role of humans as the cause have been disseminated from the recent administration; however, new information is now rushing out to the public through every media channel. The price of a barrel of oil continues at record levels, affecting prices in every global sector. The American dollar and indeed American ideals are at an all-time low. People are feeling or seeing firsthand the effects of climate change: the melting of the ice caps, the loss of habitat for thousands of varieties of plants and animals, and the increased severity of the weather over the past decade. We're in a perfect storm for introducing options for significant change in our society. The old way was to target an offending company and litigate against it to change its behavior and for punitive damages—mostly led by regional environmental activist organizations. Now, these same offender businesses are taking another look at sustainability because it may be in their financial interests to do so. That's not necessarily the noblest reason, but it's a start. Since there is more push than pull in the marketplace toward sustainability, there is a need to help inspire and guide enterprises toward higher ground. The perfect storm of environmental, social, and economic circumstances pressuring individuals and companies provides a unique opportunity for normally contentious groups to join forces and effect meaningful change.

To illustrate this point: While working in sub-Saharan Africa over a three-year period, I noticed the difference between the nonprofit development organizations spending their limited-budget funds and the for-profit entities striving to survive in a difficult economic environment. Among the issues facing countries dependent upon foreign aid for infrastructure development, medicine, and other societal basics is the dependence on the foreign aid in the first place. Even if the grant-funded nonprofits help train local citizens to take over key positions, continued funding is still required to sustain the organization—but it is not guaranteed forever. Too many projects are completed without expertise, administration, and funding left behind to continue the work once the developmental funding dries up. For-profit entities look at solving problems through a different lens, that of finding a market that is able to financially sustain products and services sufficiently without dependence on external grants. This requires rethinking the cost of these goods and services in relation to the local economy; but more hurdles can be overcome by entrepreneurial planning than by budgetary planning alone. I found that the best of both worlds was to form public/private alliances to achieve greater goals of expertise, infrastructure, administration, and sustainability appropriate to the local economy. In like manner, I believe the public/private alliances that can be formed by the non-profit environmental activist groups, social change organizations, and economic development organizations with regional companies will help generate a spark of ideas, better outcomes from joint initiatives, and, most important, financial sustainability in the long run.

FROM THE GOLD RUSH TO THE GREEN RUSH

During another era in the United States, the young country was in the process of westward expansion into the frontier. Linking the two coasts together were the railroads and another new technology: the telegraph. On May 23, 1844, a message, "What hath God wrought?" was quietly tapped out across a wire miles away that unceremoniously opened the dawn of a new age—that of innovation and industry. But the message was also a call to a higher purpose since the world had become smaller with the symbolic flattening of mountains and drying of the seas. Similarly today, the Internet began as an arcane transmission of text messages between engineers and has grown to connect individuals globally to an extent previously inconceivable. Ironically, a year before the first telegraph message, the U.S. Patent Office reduced its staff and budget in the belief at the time that no new inventions were likely to be made. Little did anyone realize that an explosion of inventions was about to occur that would transform every aspect of people's lives and fuel the development of technology and systems for the industrial revolution.

The discovery of gold in California in 1849 attracted an influx of fortune-seekers from all over the world, and many did strike it rich; but the greatest impact was the connecting the industrial center of the East to the vast, untapped resources of the West by railroad and the rapid development of industries and communities with the new-found wealth. By the time the gold dried up and the dream of getting rich quick was gone, the new economy of the West was well on its way to unlimited growth from other industries. The entrepreneurial spirit brought freedom-seeking individuals from all over the world to the United States to fulfill a dream of self-sufficiency, of owning land and farming it, and of building businesses. Entrepreneurs tend to thrive in a down economy. It has been during difficult financial times that most of the successful companies were born, as their visionary leaders had to innovate or move on.

After the Civil War, the industrial complex in the United States that we still benefit from today was in an exponential growth mode. Vast resources were extracted—from the old-growth forests to the coal mines in Appalachia and iron ore from the West—to fuel the expansion of cities and industries that would produce the wealthiest nation in the world within a few short decades. By the early 1900s, the country's citizens were becoming consumers with an insatiable appetite for the new American dream: unchecked growth in wealth, home and land ownership, a car in every garage, inexpensive fuel and energy, and an ever-growing catalog of goods to purchase. Not until health concerns and lakes burning from toxins put the brakes on this illusion of unlimited access to resources and growth did the country get notice to regulate and curb this growth.

Unfortunately, few industries took the high road on their own to limit their growth and negative environmental and social impact.

In the 1960s, the first inklings of concerns about the end of oil, climate change, population growth, and ozone depletion were being introduced to mostly deaf ears. The rest of the world has begun to scale up their industrial complexes, especially India and China, and the pressure is on to meet the increased demand. Now we as a global community have reached an impasse. In 1999, in answer to a previous age of industrialism, Amory Lovins, L. Hunter Lovins, and Paul Hawkins' seminal book, *Natural Capitalism*, outlined "The Next Industrial Revolution," in which "limits to prosperity are coming to be determined by natural capital [water, minerals, oil, trees, fish, soil, air, etc.] rather than industrial prowess."[8]

The economic implication for investors, entrepreneurs, and companies that take notice of the shift in the need for new energy solutions is that they will benefit from a potential trillion-dollar energy market. In their book, *Earth: The Sequel—The Race to Reinvent Energy and Stop Global Warming*, Fred Krupp and Miriam Horn outline the means of "the reindustrialization of the whole planet" through innovations in green technologies—reducing energy consumption, increasing energy storage and transfer, and discovering new energy sources.[9] Now there is both a crisis and an opportunity for the business community to become aware of its critical role in helping to define the principles and to take positive action for a more sustainable world. Former adversaries are now uniting to solve the greatest challenge of our time; and by all indications, like the forty-niners during the Gold Rush, the eco-entrepreneur is at the spear point.

EVIDENCE OF THE GREEN RUSH

So how do we know that sustainability is not just a fad and that once the pressure is off, once gas prices go back to a "reasonable" $3 per gallon, who's to say that we Americans won't slip back into our old ways of indifferent consumerism? It has happened before—for example, during the previous oil crisis of the 1970s, I recall my parents waiting in the lines at gas pumps, the reduction of the speed limit to 55 mph, and the advice to turn out lights when not in use. Many new green technologies such as efficient solar cells and wind turbines for collecting energy were started. But by the mid-1980s, green was virtually forgotten. The industrial complex expanded faster and farther than ever. The cost of gas at one point in the 1990s was so low, it was comparatively the same price allowing for inflation as in the early 1900s! By the end of the twentieth century, though, something had changed. There was more physical evidence that perhaps climate change was real, that our energy sources were more limited than we had thought, and that our economy was more vulnerable to global events and other counties' economies than we had realized. For entrepreneurs, business managers, and investors, the best evidence is what is actually happening on the ground. The concept of "Smart Green" is designed to look beyond the media messages, the marketing ploys, and celebrity endorsements.

You could always count on the media reporting on green issues during the period around Earth Day in April, until 2008 when it seemed Earth Day was every day. During the early part of the year it started: Headlines were abundant on new technologies, the need for innovation, worries about climate changes, and the new green labor markets coming about. No sooner were innovative eco-entrepreneurs creating the next efficient photovoltaic cell in their garages and boosting the gas mileage of their Priuses with laptop batteries than the media began reporting on consumer "green fatigue" and the looming "green bubble." The media's role is a double-edged sword. On one hand, it has the power to inform and inspire innovations in green technology and actions individuals and companies can take to become greener, but on the other hand it reports on how interest in sustainability is waning—from all the negative news about the slump in sales for gas-guzzling SUVs to the growing of algae in your pond to fuel your car. What gets lost is the real message about sustainability, the big picture of climate change and its effects on our daily lives, and the opportunity we have to do something about it in a meaningful way.

If sustainability is already a goal and a mission for you, great. For those of you who are skeptical, that's great, too. All I ask is for you to take a broader look outside of your familiar sector and analyze the trend for yourself. Run the numbers for investment. Observe consumer behavior. Follow the money.

GREEN INVESTING

During this "early" period of the rise of green technology or green tech, the bulk of the investments being made are for the big win in replacing energy sources such as solar photovoltaics, wind turbines, biofuels, and fuel cells. According to world-renowned venture capitalist and environmental advocate, John Doerr, there is no chance of over-investing in green tech: "The energy market is $6 trillion. I like to say it's the mother of all markets. Compared to the Internet, which is a big deal, this is much bigger, much more exciting," he said. "But the challenge is much larger. Going green—solving that problem will be largest transformation on the planet." Even though green tech has seen the largest increase in investment over the past few years, Doerr believes there is still a long way to go.[10]

The trend is accelerating at a rapid pace: Venture capitalists in the U.S. invested $2.7 billion or 9 percent of their portfolios in 2006 in the clean-energy sector up from 0.6 percent in 2000! In just one year between 2006-2007, new global investments in energy technologies increased by 60 percent. In spite of these significant increases in green tech so far, these gains fall short of the $16 trillion needed to be invested by 2030 (or about $600 billion per year) to meet the growth in projected demand for new electricity and fuel sources worldwide, according to The International Energy Agency, an intergovernmental body focused on energy policy.[11] Also, it's not clear how the recent economic downturn will affect the trends and levels of investment into green tech. As the chart indicates below, the energy markets are expected to diversify and rise significantly as follows:

SIZE OF THE OPPORTUNITY

$500 billion   Value of low-carbon energy markets by 2050 (Stern Report)

$100 billion   Demand for projects generating greenhouse gases (GHG) emissions credits by 2030 (United Nations)

$100 billion	Worldwide investment in clean energy by 2009 (New Energy Finance)
$18.6–$23.1 billion	Estimated solar industry revenues by 2010 (Solar Buzz)
$15 billion	Global fuel cell and distributed hydrogen market by 2015 (Climate Group)
$84 billion	Cumulative net savings from energy-efficient products in United States by 2012 (Climate Group)

Source: Deutsche Bank, "Investing in Climate Change," October 2007.

The investment community is making it clear that there is an enormous emerging market in green tech or clean tech that will far surpass the peak investment levels of the dot-com era, and that green has moved from an interest of environmentalists to the mainstream, only now with life on our planet at stake.

THE NEW ENVIRONMENTALISM

American consumers are more knowledgeable today about climate change, which is pressuring companies to adapt or lose out on this growing market trend. Rapid access to diverse information on the Internet has spurred this change, but there is also an increase in genuine concern about products on the part of the consumer. They will ask, "Where did this product come from?" "How was it made?" "How was it shipped?" "How will it be disposed of?" and so on. Ron Pernick of Clean Edge reflected that "We're no longer at the stage where people need to be introduced to these issues; we're at a stage where people are asking below-the-surface questions, devising innovative remedies, and creating new business plans to address some of the greatest challenges of our time: resource constraints, environmental degradation, energy security, and economic and job creation."[12]

A recent U.S. National Technology Readiness Survey (NTRS)[13] found that 71 percent of adults are interested in green technology. "About half of that is in transportation technologies, like hybrid vehicles, biofuels, and energy-saving vehicles—about $50 billion worth." Solar home heating comes in at the No. 2 spot in the survey, with a market potential of $20.6 billion. Other technologies that could get a piece of the potential action according to the survey are home automation systems for things like lighting, heating, ventilation, and air-conditioning, as well as solar water heaters, home water purification, high-efficiency cooling, high-efficiency heating, and energy-saving lightbulbs—"things that just support a green lifestyle."[14] To meet this demand, companies are increasing their budgets to accommodate consumer interest and demand for green products and sustainable companies. A study in 2007 by the Aberdeen Group demonstrates significant growth in retailers going green.[15] Moreover, 75 percent of enterprises have green-dedicated budgets that will remain the same or increase in the 2008–2009 time period and lists the six key focus areas for retailers indicated in the following chart:[16]

* Adopt enterprise-wide policies for green sourcing/procurement (59 percent)
* Institute eco-friendly mandates for waste management (54 percent)
* Institute eco-friendly mandates around packaging (48 percent)
* Redesign the retail supply chain to align with green/responsible mandates (41 percent)
* Offer eco-friendly end-of-life product programs to customers (41 percent)
* Redesign store facilities and infrastructure around sustainability goals (35 percent)

Companies are becoming more aware of a more demanding class of the socially minded customer and are increasing investments by an average of 22 percent to meet the new demand. These customers seek out information and share it with others virally via the Internet; they are more involved with issues and are less passive shoppers; they produce content themselves and want flexibility from suppliers of products and services.[17] At a recent conference for facilities managers, a vendor selling roofing tiles for a 30-year-old company told me how the company had redesigned its product to be less harmful to the environment. He described how they had to redefine what a roof is. This is fascinating, because if every company stopped to consider the definition and meaning of what it makes—a roof is an energy creator, a heat deflector, a garden, a protector from the elements, a rain collector, a beautiful design—our world would quickly become more sustainable. Think about what a car is. What is a building? We can redefine everything in terms of its function, purpose, design, and contribution to the web of life: Power companies will provide energy efficiency and low or zero carbon-emission energy sources (solar, wind, and geothermal power), rather than just cheap and reliable electricity. Instead of building inefficient structures, architects will design "living structures" that reuse water, that utilize significantly less energy or produce excess energy, and that are cleaner, brighter, and healthier. Garbage collectors will transform landfills as energy and fertilizer producers and sources of recycled and reused products instead of creating another landfill.

The roofing vendor said the business was thriving because of the CEO's foresight to see the trend toward sustainability four years earlier. According to IBM in its "Global CEO Study", the largest study of chief executives ever conducted, reveals that CEOs reported a surprising level of optimism about change as an opportunity to build new competitive advantage. Overall, "83 percent of surveyed CEOs expect substantial change in the future, an increase of 28 percent in just two years." The roofing company is now creating roofing materials that are not petroleum based and can be disposed of without harm to the environment. This new environmentalism is now dependent upon innovative, motivated entrepreneurs, green managers, consumers, and investors willing to see the financial opportunity and have a vision for a sustainable future. "The shift won't happen overnight; neither is it a fait accompli. Instead, it will take a concerted effort among enlightened policy makers, technologists, entrepreneurs, business titans, academics, financiers, citizens, and others over the next 10 to 20 years."[18]

The road before the global community to become more sustainable may not be clear, but the imperative to change and adapt in the face of challenging conditions is becoming clearer every day. Far-thinking entrepreneurs have the advantage of seeing these challenges as opportunities. Strategic planning in this evolving business climate transcends innovation and financial growth to include environmental stewardship and social equity. The next chapter discusses the first step toward thinking about the nature of this shift of thinking.

2

Taking the First Step— Becoming Aware

Only when the clamor of the outside world is silenced will you be able to hear the deeper vibration. Listen carefully.

—*Sarah Ban Breathnach*

To change and to change for the better are two different things.

—*German proverb*

OPENING THE DOOR

One thing you can count on when speaking with seasoned entrepreneurs—they will be both optimistic and brutally practical at the same time. As a veteran of entrepreneurship since 1994 with all my successes and failures, I consider each of my ventures as leading toward a better approach for the next time. This makes me insatiably optimistic about my prospects, but it also makes me extremely practical and task-oriented. Many of the business owners interviewed for this book were asked a series of questions about going green and thinking about sustainability; each of them was polite, to the point, committed, and always focused on the practicalities of keeping a business going. At the General Store Café in Pittsboro, North Carolina, owner/partner/manager Vance Remick laughed when I asked him what his motivations were for his sustainability strategies. "First of all," he said, "it's about the marketability of our product to our customers. I believe it's the right thing to do, my customers expect it, and I feel responsible to our investors who also expect it. But we can't do everything we'd like to do, because of cost and time. It's a delicate balance——between keeping our doors open and keeping customers and investors happy." Down the road a spell, Mark Estill, co-founder of Piedmont Biofuels Industrial LLC, is very dedicated to the cause of living lightly on the earth, but at the same time very aware of the physical realities of running a successful business. He defines sustainability as being able to live in concert with the environment. Asked why he and his brother, Lyle Estill, author of *Living Local*, started the company, he stated matter-of-factly, "We anticipated a trend in the increase of petroleum prices, developed a method to replace diesel with something more environmentally-friendly, and in the process, we make some cash."

What is this relationship between entrepreneurship and sustainability? The qualities necessary to be successful in business are similar to many of those that support a more sustainable enterprise. Most business leaders will agree that among the most important qualities to be successful in business, entrepreneurs must have integrity, be truthful and honest, have an inner drive to succeed, be willing to take risks, be innovative and resourceful, and my favorite: be able to design their future with vision, research, and hard work. Some would call this luck.

THE ENTREPRENEURIAL SPIRIT

Entrepreneurs have an incredibly important role to play in the move toward sustainability and the reduction of the effects of climate change. If you include all the small business owners and start-ups, entrepreneurs contribute over 50 percent to the U.S. gross domestic product (GDP)[1] and 97 percent of jobs for companies with less than 500 employees (50 percent of jobs for the private sector).[2] Most innovations that we enjoy today—from telephones to computers—are derived not from well-funded research labs but from entrepreneurs taking a risk, working hard, and persevering with the belief that you can create your own destiny. When I speak of successful entrepreneurs, I'm actually speaking of the entrepreneurial spirit that can be found in each one of us in each of our roles or functions, whether we are a consumer, a bank manager, a scholar, an investor, or an eco-entrepreneur. The entrepreneurial spirit encompasses attitudes and actions people take beyond what is expected of them and what other people may think of them, and can appear in any person in any role. The unique difference, though, between the spirit of the entrepreneur found in all people and spirit of the entrepreneur who embarks on his or her own journey with new ideas and a new company is the compulsion to explore and be independent.

My own experience of building companies has given me a clearer view of what it takes to be a successful entrepreneur—a never-ending learning process. Before I started my first business, I worked in the adult literacy field with Volunteers in Service to America (VISTA), in South America, and for five years at a not-for-profit organization called Literacy South that improves the quality of learning and results of literacy programs and teachers throughout the Southeast. Every year I was growing professionally: I was planning and delivering training to teachers, supporting and facilitating writing campaigns, writing articles, and publishing a student journal. Though we accomplished a lot, I was not earning enough money to support my growing family and keep up with changes in the economy. I was receiving increasing requests for moonlighting jobs designing and writing newsletters for other nonprofits, and so I left Literacy South to form my own company. My dad, who is also an entrepreneur, said to me that once I started on this journey to expect change, and like a virus, new ideas and opportunities would infect my brain and compel me to adapt. Shortly afterward, I attended a technology conference and sampled access to something called the World Wide Web using a browser called Mosaic. I suddenly saw the future in combining the power of the Web with proven adult education principles to provide high-quality, Web-based educational programs at lower cost for more people. My new e-learning company was born. Based on my own experience and after communicating with dozens of other entrepreneurs, I learned about the attributes of the entrepreneurial spirit. They are many, but I have reduced them to seven:

1. *See a need to fill.* Entrepreneurs have the ability to recognize a need in the marketplace and develop a product or service to fill it. Regardless of whether the product or service already exists, a successful entrepreneur finds a way to improve upon it, make it cheaper, or come up with an entirely new approach.

2. *Be a self-starter and be independent.* Entrepreneurs by nature are compelled to strike out on their own and do it their own way. Successful entrepreneurs know the value of mentors and choosing good people to work with them, but the vision, direction, and leadership role is still theirs.

3. *Desire to grow financially.* Entrepreneurs start businesses because they have the ability not only to fulfill a dream of developing something out of nothing and have their vision realized in what they love to do in life, but also to grow a business financially. Successful entrepreneurs utilize financial resources wisely to achieve two of the most important metrics: financial sustainability and return on investment (ROI).

4. *Thrive with change.* Entrepreneurs know that to be effective in their business, they need to adapt to changes in the marketplace very quickly, either to meet the changing demands of their customers or to stay a few steps ahead of their competition. Successful entrepreneurs are always looking around corners to anticipate potential dangers and opportunities requiring periodic assessment of their goals, objectives, and tasks as they relate to financial outcomes.

5. *Make connections that others don't see.* Entrepreneurs have the uncanny ability to make connections and draw conclusions in creative ways that make it possible for them to be innovators and risk takers. Successful entrepreneurs are able to profitably transform seemingly disparate information and processes into practical approaches for development and delivery of their products and services.

6. *Be driven to persevere under all conditions.* Entrepreneurs are tenacious and persistent in the most adverse conditions when everyone else has given up. Successful entrepreneurs are aware of differences between seeing a company through tough times and closing up shop or adapting to another approach. They know when to hold 'em and when to fold 'em.

7. *Be keenly aware of your own strengths and weaknesses.* Entrepreneurs are able to self-assess who they are, what are they are good at, and what they know they can't do. Successful entrepreneurs lead their companies with their strengths and hire talented people to cover their weaknesses.

Many successful entrepreneurs I've had the privilege of learning from have indicated that they are committed to what they do because they are compelled to do so and because they have a greater purpose in mind to try to improve upon what others have done before them— to leave their mark on the world by making it just a little better. This commitment to a vision that drives some entrepreneurs to the brink of oblivion—I know, I've been there—is the bridge to the drastic changes of mind-set and action required in response to many of the global changes in climate and resources that are increasingly becoming critical.

SUSTAINABILITY AND ENTREPRENEURSHIP

As mentioned in the previous chapter, the Green Rush is already on, but it is just the beginning. The attraction of trillion-dollar energy markets, the gap between products and services widening with the increase of green consumers concerned about how and where things are made, and the increased interest from investors who see the trend represent all the pull necessary to attract new and existing entrepreneurs to begin filling the gap. However, it's the attribute of the entrepreneur to make connections that few others ever see that is the most important push for business owners and new entrepreneurs to contribute innovation and fresh thinking to a worsening problem.

Other traditional players from the environmental and social change community, including organizers, activists, scientists, and policy makers, need to recognize that those in the business community, especially entrepreneurs, are critical team members for the changes and innovations required to combat the effects of climate change, global warming, depleted food and manufacturing resources, and the end of oil, and address concerns about conservation, biodiversity, and human health. Once considered the nemesis of all things environmental, the business community is no longer the target of litigation for change but an essential partner in an overall system of change.

At a recent forum bringing together both public and private organizations to share their views about and uniting their efforts for a more sustainable community, one executive described a company's experience in reaching across the public/private divide by transforming an investment property into a valuable wetland. A developer completing a mixed-use housing development had a toxic waste dump to contend with. The developer's choices were to cover it with blacktop or convert it to a wetland; a small public/private consortium of advisers promised to write the developer a check for $100,000 if it agreed to the latter course. The consortium cleaned up the swamp, transformed it into a bird and amphibian sanctuary, and handed the developer the promised check. Not only that—the developer's property values increased due to the proximity of the newly transformed wetland!

All over the country, traditional adversaries are joining forces for potential mutual benefit. In Oregon, the timber companies and environmentalists have formed some remarkable alliances for the preservation and conservation of forests and wildlife. A former president of the Sierra Club, Adam Werbach, left his post to found an environmental consulting firm, and took on as a client one of his main adversaries, Wal-Mart, much to the chagrin of many Sierra Club members.[3] But now some changes to distribution, energy efficiency, product offerings, and local produce, just to name a few, are beginning to emerge in Wal-Mart stores across the country. In this case, joining the retailer and effecting change from within is better than fighting it from without.

The most recent annual forum of the Alliance for Regional Stewardship (ARS), the nation's premier peer-to-peer network of civic entrepreneurs working to build vibrant, globally competitive regional communities, demonstrated through the presentations of individual members and regional teams that success in their regions is dependent upon the quality of the public/private relationships. On a smaller scale, companies are joining forces with local nonprofits, environmental groups, agricultural cooperatives, and community organizers to strike a balance between realizing a vision for sustainability and attracting more business. Going back to the General Store Café in Pittsboro, North Carolina, the owners realized the advantages of hosting burrito dinner fund-raisers for different nonprofit organizations— on slow nights—rather than donating $25 gift certificates to them. The Monday night Burrito Bash is now booked solid for 42 weeks a year, each with a different nonprofit benefiting from the Café's proceeds. Meanwhile, the Café enjoys a packed house with potential new customers from around the region sampling the food and likely to return with more customers on other days. "Social equity builds traffic," said Vance. "I'm driven by this concept of marketability, but I also feel responsible to the community." In addition to the Burrito Bash, the Café displays local art for sale, supports local growers, participates as a board member on the local Arts Council, and contributes to the annual Relay for Life and Haw River Festival events.

The Chapel Hill Chamber of Commerce, though a nonprofit organization, serves the business community beyond the normal charter of providing a source of leads, resources, and advocacy to encourage thriving local businesses. The president, Aaron Nelson, realized that the trend toward sustainability in the community was a global megatrend and that the organization could add to its charter as an inspiration to its current members and attract new members. Aaron and his board formed a subsidiary organization called the Foundation for Sustainable Community with the mission of "investing business and community resources to promote and advance the triple bottom line of community sustainability: environmental stewardship, social equity, and economic prosperity." In addition to providing access to information and opportunities for companies to network on sustainability issues regularly together, the Foundation hopes to develop a sustainability assessment tool that helps to guide companies through a progressive process of growth to become more green—a model that could be utilized by other chambers of commerce nationally. With the power of numbers of small businesses nationwide, Aaron believes this public/private partnership will leverage sustainability outcomes more successfully than other efforts, because of the impact small businesses have on jobs and revenue, as well as carbon footprint, water usage, energy efficiency, and other sustainability outcomes.

THE LURE OF SUSTAINABILITY

Why are entrepreneurs attracted to sustainable products and processes knowing that they are likely to be more expensive? Besides, it's not guaranteed that customers, investors, employees, and other stakeholders will follow; the payback period on their return on investment is uncertain; and there is no clear definition of what sustainability is, let alone what exactly the entrepreneur should be doing. I am personally committed to sustainability through changes in my actions as a consumer, a citizen of the world, and an entrepreneur. The combination of social equity, environmental stewardship, and profit speaks to my beliefs about why I'm in business in the first place. It is not a stretch to give a label to my work and learn from a global community of people striving for the same goal from a myriad of approaches. Sustainability for me provides a focus of learning and an application of principles that have not had a shared community and a common goal before. As loose as that may sound, it's similar to what I've heard from dozens of business owners across the country.

Over the course of several months, I interviewed dozens of CEOs of small to medium-sized companies across multiple sectors such as restaurants, retailers, home builders, solar panel manufacturers, banks, and community organizations. Though I was interested in how they defined sustainability and what they were doing, I was more interested to learn about the why factor. What was their mindset when considering sustainability from both personal and business perspectives? Also, how did they know if they were successful? What were the reactions from stakeholders such as customers, board members, investors, and employees? Not surprisingly, most of the business owners, even those whom I will call eco-entrepreneurs—those who have created a company specifically for sustainable products and services—were cautiously optimistic. Their markets are just emerging, but each owner described his or her own commitment to sustainability and how that translated to meeting increasing demands from customers. Most of them took steps toward becoming sustainable as a result of personal conviction that becoming sustainable is the right thing to do. They look for profitability from increasing customer demand, and long-term economic benefits from cost savings as they make changes to their own organizations. Here are a few examples of company owners and decision makers who have taken steps to become more sustainable:

Chad Ray, president of Old Heritage Builders in Wake County, North Carolina, transformed his business from a quality-focused company to a green-focused company: "I try to build in a way that will help reduce the cost of constructing and operating a building." Chad measures his outcomes by his profits: "If we are profitable doing the things we believe in, then that is a success. If I don't make a living at this, it is just a hobby. Hobbies are fine, but not for a business."

Another builder nearby, Michael Chandler of Chandler Design-Build, adds to the profitability outcome: "Our goal is to stay profitable, not working more than 40 hours a week, and have flexible time with family. We have a long-term plan to keep the company strong and healthy long into the future through employee retention, improving how the business serves its employees and the community; including employee benefits that lead to lower health care costs and working more efficiently." Michael Chandler is enthusiastic about taking care of the people who make up his business. They are family to him, and he knows that supporting them will make his business stronger: "If your employees are loyal and happy, it's good for the bottom line in the long run and good for the peace of mind for employers—mutually supportive. We hold each other to a higher standard."

Blakley Huntley of BB&T Corporation describes how "the banking industry is supportive of sustainable design and construction and helping builders who uphold the ethic of building a lasting product of high quality to be profitable and able to stay in business." She also explains that the bank's motivation to change its own internal practices towards recycling and becoming more active and in meeting the challenges in of lending to green builders and educating appraisers is in response to a growing trend in the industry. She says, "Our manager is very supportive of us, and realizing there is potentially a good market, she requested and approved us for being a pilot for the paperless program at BB&T. Our ongoing challenge remains on the appraiser side, which is highly regulated, and there is not a lot that we can do to educate them. We have been successful at getting Energy Star and green certifications of homes represented on the Triangle Multiple Listing Service so that appraisers and Realtors can better assess the property. Affordability and justifying the value of sustainability is the big challenge."

For Bradley Yoder of Triangle PolySteel, the decision to shift his attention to a more sustainable product line was one of basic economics: "I found something that fits my own worldview, which makes my motivation sustainable to do what I do. For me, it was basic economics: taking a look at the market—hard numbers—and offering a product that people want or will want." Beyond his hard look at the bottom line, Bradley was inspired by William McDonough, a well-known architect of sustainable design and pioneer of building "good" products rather than "less bad" ones. McDonough pushes sustainability thinking by asking whether someone would want to be a part of a sustainable relationship. What fun would that be? On one hand, it will last. On another, will it be life-giving or exciting? Bradley was very clear in having a long-term plan for profitability and sustainability: "If you don't have a sustainable practice or product or plan, you're just dead in the water. I don't want to be part of a trend. The product I offer helps buildings last a long time. Having a business based on that concept will help it last rather than just be a shot in the dark."

Paul Toma, who led a building and design team for many years, came up with the idea several years ago of opening the Common Ground Green Building Center to provide alternative products for homeowners and builders in the Research Triangle area of North Carolina. His dream became a reality in early 2008 when he opened the doors to an enthusiastic crowd of customers with sustainable products such as flooring, paints, countertops, and carpets. Paul is committed to educating the community to ask the right questions: "There is a huge overall picture about which you need to ask questions and see what pieces of the puzzle are covered by the product for it to be considered sustainable. A lot of products say they are sustainable, but people don't know what that means—they could be cutting down old-growth forests and considering wood a renewable resource." The founders changed their own personal practices, which evolved into the desire to become eco-entrepreneurs: "We started a sustainable company that sells all environmentally-friendly building materials, bought a Prius, and purchased a biodiesel truck for deliveries, and installed a solar water heater; we reduce our use of resources, and buy organic and local products. Basically, we are trying to live a sustainable lifestyle on as many levels as we can—within reason." Paul mentioned that he has faith in the changes he sees happening in the media and that there is more awareness of the global problems: "The coolest thing about what's going on now is that it is all right in front of you. The media is focusing a lot on green—maybe some people still don't know what that means, but more people are talking about it and are open to it. Everyone is so keyed in to the movement—or at least aware of what is going on—that they are more likely to adopt changes. The best part of this business is that we are having an unbelievable response. There are a lot of really great, educated, passionate people here who are demanding our services."

Most of the business owners and managers I spoke with knew when they started they were taking a risk, but there was consistently a clear sense of commitment that they knew it was going to take time; that not everyone is going to get it, though most eventually will; and that it starts with changing yourself first, learning what you need to know, and then taking small steps forward. Everyone's road to sustainability is going to be different, some taking giant leaps forward and others very small, almost imperceptible steps, and it is my belief that it's best to build a fire on hot coals. In the well-known model about the five stages of change, it's useful to place your decisions and those around you in a framework and to understand the mind-set and actions necessary to move from one stage to another.[4]

The first stage is *pre-contemplation*. People in this stage are not aware or choose not to acknowledge there is a problem. Their actions and behaviors are potentially destructive to themselves and to others without their knowing.

The second stage is *contemplation*. People in this stage have become aware that there is a problem and that changes in their behavior need to take place, but they are not ready to take action. Many people remain for long periods of time in this stage.

The third stage is *pre-action*. A person is this stage has moved from being aware of the problem to now being more informed and desiring to take action. This is often considered the tipping point for many individuals' realization that a problem has existed, and they have a newfound desire to change. Individuals have many false starts toward action in this stage because of the potential risks of failure.

The fourth stage is *action*. People in this stage take all that they have learned and their desire for change and take steps toward changing their behavior. Since it is early in their process, many people recycle to earlier stages.

The fifth stage is *maintenance*. People in this stage have taken action and have experienced positive results propelling them forward to continue taking this action. Fewer people in this stage recycle through other stages, and more of them are considered to have experienced change.

In the context of change toward sustainability, many business owners mentioned that they experienced the stage where they were unaware or unwilling to change their behavior. Business demands and a lack of understanding of the implications of their actions prevented them from learning more or considering any form of change in their lives or businesses. Most business owners, in fact, were already practicing some form of cost containment for energy, were recycling and reusing materials when it cost more to do otherwise, and were providing better pay and benefits to retain good people. They were pre-contemplative about sustainability but were taking action in recycling for conservation or in social equity and were in maintenance for paying their employees a living wage. But this did not connect for them to a greater cause that would have an impact on global warming or depleted resources, or indicate that a broader, systemic viewpoint to their behavior could potentially increase their business and have a positive effect on the environment. Not until there was a customer requesting a green product or other outside influence did they begin the process of moving out of the contemplation stage to pre-action. Table 2.1 illustrates the stages business owners could be in for various issues in relation to a few activities leading to a more sustainable model.

Table 2.1   Stages of Change. An example of how a company's sustainable activities can be in several stages at once.

Stage of Change	Sustainable Activity Sample
Pre-Contemplative (Unaware)	The company's products are made from a toxic chemical that is a known carcinogen.
Contemplative (Aware but Inactive)	Competing companies are beginning to reduce their carbon emissions and the CEO can't imagine his company doing the same.
Pre-Action (Ready for Action)	The company has developed a business case and set a date to establish a profit sharing plan.
Action (Taking Action in Small Steps)	The company has offered employees the opportunity to work at least one week at home per month to save on fuel.
Maintenance (Sustained Action)	The company has been recycling paper, cardboard, bottles, and cans for 3 years.

As you can see in this chart, it is possible to have some actions in the maintenance stage of change but others in earlier stages. Being aware of this helps the business owner determine possible next steps for moving from one stage to another and avoid recycling through earlier stages. During the earlier stages of contemplation and pre-action, it's easy to stand on the sidelines and watch as others take the risks and succeed or fail. The Green Rush that the world is experiencing at this moment is gathering momentum, and as in the industrial revolution and information age before it, those who miss the opportunity will be left in the dust. The first few actions are always the hardest, because you may have to invest capital, there may not be widespread support or may even be ridicule from stakeholders, and the effort may actually fail. What matters most is taking the first step and realizing that there is low-hanging fruit to grab that establishes business value for your organization with minimal effort; there will then be a growing community of support to spark new ideas and encourage your progress.

Perhaps you have reached the point of contemplation in learning more about how to begin a sustainability strategy but have not absorbed enough information to take action. You may have had a tipping point for the desire to change but want to go green in a way that doesn't match your ability to sustain the effort, or perhaps your customers consider you to be greenwashing—marketing yourself as green without really being green. If you are ready to embark on this journey, it's best to have a well-laid-out plan—a sustainability strategy—in the form of a long-term business case that encompasses all of the stages of change you will pass through and the guideposts along the way to ensure the roads you will take will get you to where you want to go. By deciding to begin the journey to develop a sustainability strategy, you have taken the first step toward becoming a *Smart Green* company.

WHAT IS A SMART GREEN COMPANY?

A Smart Green company has the same basic elements of a company becoming more sustainable, with a little bit more. There is no clear definition of what sustainability is for everyone, because it will constantly change depending on your understanding of the level of the crisis, as well as who, when, and where you are in your community, region, or country, or anywhere in the world. However, you can be *smart* about the balance between your behavior, your company's actions, and the impacts (positive and negative) you are having on society and the environment. Although there are now hundreds of certification programs available for companies to establish their level of achievement in sustainability, such as Green Seal, LEED, Cradle to Cradle, and ISO 14000, a Smart Green company signifies applying your skills and talents as an entrepreneur to see a need, design and develop a product or service, and measure your results, and realizing the vision of success for your company—striking the balance between entrepreneurship and sustainability.

BECOMING A SMART GREEN COMPANY

Becoming a Smart Green company requires a process of change. The first step toward change of your organization is to start change with yourself through reflection, education, networking, and saving costs. Paulo Nery, owner of PracticalEco, and writer/editor for *Footprint* magazine, defines sustainability as "leaving the world as good as we found it—or ideally a little better." Paulo goes on to say, "The word I have been using recently to describe what sustainability requires of us and how to incorporate it into our lives is *Mindful*. For me, it underlines the fact that there are no magic bullets—that by looking after the little things and paying attention to the impact of small actions you begin to make a difference. Of course, these days I've cut back on driving—even with a Prius. That's a sacrifice sometimes because I'd prefer to meet with people in person, but I do business on the phone as much as possible. In the end, there are balances to be struck in everything you do, and being mindful of your impact is essential. It simply means we are more conscious about what we do. That sort of thinking should apply at all levels—personal, commercial and civic."

Tom VanZeeland, territory executive of RainEscape™, which provides rain-collection systems, Aquaeras™, for homes and businesses, shared changes he made in his company that stem from his personal conviction that "sustainability is a product or by-product that has the ability to regenerate itself so that it has no impact on the environment from where it started." For his own company, Tom started recycling in his office, changed his delivery and freight transportation to hybrid cars, and began exploring how he can provide products that are created with less harmful materials to the environment. The first step is reflection.

Reflection

Ask simple questions to reflect on, such as the following five examples:

1. How do I define going green?

2. What are the tipping points for me to consider changing my behavior toward going green?

3. Where can I get practical information about meaningful change in my daily life for going green?

4. How will I prevent myself from recycling back to an earlier stage of behavior change, such as contemplation (no action)?

5. What are my risks and benefits of becoming more sustainable?

Your answers to these questions are meant to be for your own benefit. They will change as you become more aware of the issues, find out what's possible to be done, and acquire better information about the impact of your actions.

Education

By creating a library of information for yourself, it soon becomes a valuable resource to educate stakeholders, management staff, employees, and potential customers. Bill Rouse, Green Products Specialist of Stock Building Supply, describes the educational process as it began disseminating throughout his organization: "Staff just started getting on board. Corporate has been getting on board with more people coming in to educate our staff, taking classes in building green. Some vendors are ahead of us, putting out the literature, using recycled products, trying to outdo each other. More than sustainability, they are trying to reach and hold their niche. As a company we try to work with our builders and have them bring the customers in. Management has really come on board, sitting down weekly with us to educate themselves."

Michele Myers of M-Squared Builders and Designers is very passionate about green building, efficient and healthy homes. She is very active in the Home Builders Association's green building council (at the local and state level) to promote green building as the way to go for North Carolina, and Orange County in particular. Continuous education of vendors, subcontractors, and staff about green products and processes has been key to her company's success: "Vendors have been so happy and open in getting me the information [and about] using their products. The subcontractors have been good if you explain what is necessary. The contractors who get it save on costs of building. Our staff is enjoying learning new things. It gets easier every year to build green homes. Every major company and even smaller ones now have someone who can talk with you about green products. The market has started changing their thinking about water and energy. Even indoor air quality is a huge issue. We are inundated with green from the mass media, but the market is still not 100 percent there. Now I have clients that are requesting solar, and they absolutely have to have geothermal—with the means to do it. Only since this past year are people requesting and able to pay for the green products."

Learn about the issues and concerns by taking the following steps:

1. *Become green-aware.* Start a simple personal library and read books, articles, and bookmarks from the Internet on the basics of climate change, global warming, energy, sustainability, and going green (see suggested readings in the Appendix at the end of this book).

2. *Become bio-aware.* Learn about where you live from an environmental perspective, including annual rainfall, waterways, landforms,

weather patterns, flora and fauna, agricultural zone, air quality, groundwater tables, change initiatives, and so on (see additional bio-aware items with potential sources and organizations at the end of this book).

3. *Become socially aware.* Learn about who lives near you and what kinds of issues and opportunities the community in which you live has to offer, including cultural diversity, literacy rates, changes in income over time, crime rates, birth and death rates, employment, economic growth, support organizations, change initiatives, and so on (see additional socially aware items with potential sources and organizations at the end of this book).

4. *Become energy-aware.* Learn about energy sources, usage, and impacts on air, land, water, human health, ecology, and the economy. Find out about initiatives available to improve the diversity of energy sources, incentives for change, new technologies available, and so on (see additional energy-aware items with potential sources and organizations at the end of this book).

5. *Become regionally aware.* Learn about those issues that will affect the region for the next 5, 10, 20, and 50 years based on changes in population, transportation, energy, water, land, urban sprawl, pollution, employment, health, and so on (see additional regionally aware items with potential sources and organizations at the end of this book).

Networking

Michele Myers describes how she connects with members of the community and supports her volunteers: "We have 50 subcontractors on any given job; we are involved with people of all walks of life. I remind my clients how many mouths they are contributing to feed just by building one house. We have a tremendous outreach capacity in the community. We treat the people with respect and look for diversity and have an excellent reputation for paying our contractors right. My goal is that every house is Energy Star certified and green. It's baby steps because of the economic impact."

Barb Eichberger, founder of the LinkedIn social network called "Sustainability Working Group," believes "sustainability is a way to a future of practices that increase our awareness [of how] to stay more connected with who we are in this planetary community and how we can contribute most to positive ends within that reality in everything we do. Sustainability remains a work in progress. Many people with various experiences still need to be brought into the discussion. Sustainability exists across many domains with more than multiple definitions, operational possibilities, and values, such as business, industry, commercial, retail, government, agriculture, non-profit, education. They all have interests and ideas related to ways to contribute to sustainable practices, processes, and operations."

Become part of both the local and national communities of committed individuals like yourself by taking the following five actions:

1. Join the local chamber of commerce, if you haven't already done so, and look for staff and other members interested in green issues.

2. Seek out and network with other organizations that connect businesses, universities, nonprofit organizations, and local government on the issues of going green and sustainability. When beginning your networking and exploration of resources, be very clear that you are in the early stages of planning and that you are seeking ideas, support, and additional people with whom to network.

3. Join a select group of organizations supporting green initiatives that you can be active in. This group should not be greater than three organizations in the first year. Use the opportunity to meet with others, learn from them, and gain a better understanding of the issues, constraints, and opportunities with public/private collaborations.

4. Join an online social networking group on green entrepreneurship or sustainable businesses through sites such as Facebook, LinkedIn, and MySpace. There are thousands of groups forming

around a variety of issues that you can learn from and share your ideas with.

5. Subscribe to a couple of blogs and podcasts that focus on green and sustainable issues. You receive more feedback and extend your network further if you actively post on others' blogs and podcasts. If you are ambitious, you can start your own blog and begin posting a periodic update of your own learnings to share with others. (See the end of the book for a more comprehensive list of potential networking sources and ideas.)

Cost Savings

Find the best ways to save costs while going green.

As an individual, there are dozens of opportunities for you to begin going green while finding financial justifications. More books and online resources are available now than ever to encourage individuals, families, and small businesses to begin going green. Begin the process of creating financial justifications of why you choose one green activity over another. Sustainability includes the ability to continue your behavior change beyond action and through maintenance. Create a table of actions for going green and potential cost savings for those activities. Start small and work up. Use the savings from one activity to fund other more expensive activities. Table 2.2 is a sample cost/benefit chart for going green with a short list of easy actions you can use as a template with big impact that can be implanted in both your home and business location.

People change their behaviors for many reasons, but the stages they go through are relatively consistent. The Green Rush we are experiencing on a global scale is moving the hearts and minds of people to consider the actions we are taking as individuals and communities that affect each other not only today but for generations to come. Once you have begun the process of reflecting on your motives and reasons for moving from the contemplative stage of change to being ready for action, you can then begin educating yourself on the variety of issues that affect you, your business, and the community. By networking with others, you gain a community of like-minded individuals with whom to share ideas and mentors to guide your progress.

Table 2.2   Sample Cost/Benefit Chart for Sustainability

Sustainability Strategy	Potential Cost Savings
Recycle, Reduce, Reuse. The stand-by slogan for some of the easiest activities available for going green.	Savings could be significant in choices being made in reduction of materials and reusing others for as long as possible.
Seal your space. Includes cleaning and sealing your ducts, sealing windows, switching to double-pane windows, adding window coverings, seal the chimney, add more insulation, change the insulation, seal the crawlspace.	Could realize up to 40% savings on energy usage per year, depending on the changes made.
Change automobile behavior. Some options include drive less, driver slower, use a bike or moped, carpool, buy an economy car, keep an old car.	Gas savings, new car savings.
Improve energy efficiency. Add solar panels, wind, or geothermal options. Switch to more efficient appliances, heating/AC, and water heater, change shower heads.	Energy bill savings could be 10–50%.
Collect rain. Use rain catchment for use in landscaping.	If part of city water, savings on water bill or compliance with water restriction. If on a well, less impact on ground water supply.
Buy local. Join an agricultural coop, purchase local produce, goods, and services.	Savings on food bill with the benefit of supporting local growers and producers of goods and services.

Remember that as optimistic as some ideas sound—and many business owners are optimistic—the excitement must be tempered with clarity of thought about becoming a Smart Green company. Apply your skills and talents as an entrepreneur to see a need, design and develop a product or service, and measure your results, while at the same time setting the vision of success for your company within the context of ensuring that those in the future will have the same or a better opportunity to realize their dreams.

Elena Westbrook is a former environmental consultant and continuing activist. For Westbrook, "Sustainability is one of those words that has become so popular as to lose its meaning. The original definition was a group of practices for building, manufacturing, working, or living that could be continued indefinitely without depleting resources. I've seen numerous businesses trying to label themselves as 'green' or 'sustainable' without much thought or purpose behind it. That kind of greenwashing damages everyone making an honest effort to do better." This advice is especially helpful for businesses learning about these issues for the first time.

Many CEOs are becoming active by applying many of the various principles of sustainability in their businesses, such as James F. Kenefick, founding CEO of BetterWorld Telecom, the first nationwide full-service telecommunications carrier focused on serving businesses that support social justice and sustainability: "It's great to see the way this movement toward sustainable business operations has become so mainstream over the last five years or so. Right now it's something a lot of CEOs are trying to get their arms around; figure out how it applies to them. In reality, there are entrepreneurial executives, social leaders, and environmental experts discovering new ways that businesses can be responsible citizens every day. We can't yet imagine the extent of the future interconnectivity between business, society, and the planet."

Entrepreneurs have a significant role to play in contributing to a more sustainable world. They can't do it alone, and the more that diverse communities join together, the more effective and successful their efforts and their businesses will become. Once you have taken the first steps toward sustainability, you will then be ready to proceed to the next step of action in the development and implementation of a sustainability strategic plan, presented in the next chapter.

3

Defining a Smart Green Company

We must be the change we wish to see in
the world.

—*Mahatma Gandhi*

To accomplish great things we must first dream,
then visualize, then plan . . . believe . . . act!

—*Alfred A. Montapert*

THE MOVING TARGET

You've decided to take action to go green, become sustainable. You've had your tipping point, you've reflected on the implications of the triple bottom line of sustainability, and you have determined it's more than a trend. Your business will actually thrive, or not thrive, based on your actions. But you don't want to rush into it. Though the need to change toward green practices on a personal and corporate level is urgent, business experience and wisdom remind you that "fools rush in" where patience and thoughtful planning are required. At this stage, when you are ready for action, you need to unpack the implications of a few more pieces of information before you begin. In this chapter, we explore the differences between applying sustainability principles as a Smart Green company rather than its well-intentioned but misguided opposite, a greenwashing company; discover what level of "greenth" you and your company are at and how to plan your sustainability strategy; and conduct a sustainability needs assessment. We then walk through the steps of preparing for your sustainability strategic plan by writing a mission statement and garnering buy-in from your stakeholders. By the end of this chapter, I hope you will appreciate the myriad dimensions that are at stake in your simple action to develop a plan to become a Smart Green company.

Many of the companies interviewed have provided their definitions of sustainability, most of which share variations of the internationally accepted definition from the Brundtland Report in 1987 as "development that meets the needs of the present without compromising the ability of future generations to meet their own needs." Defining sustainability takes on several more dimensions, depending on with whom you speak. This is all the more reason to accept the fact that the definition is a moving target and is determined by your own perception—your level of greenth. The following descriptions of the aspects of the triple bottom line are not definitive, but are meant to provide you with more thoughts for reflection like the diverse comments provided by the business managers and entrepreneurs earlier.

PLANTING TREES: ENVIRONMENTAL STEWARDSHIP

Environmental stewardship is the most straightforward component of the triple bottom line. It's what most people think of when they hear about a company going green or having a sustainability strategy. Environmental issues are tied directly to our understanding of the causes and effects of global warming and whether we as a collective human race can slow down those effects and prevent the most catastrophic outcomes such as higher temperatures, receding shorelines, drought, severe weather, and loss of biodiversity throughout land and sea ecosystems. The issues for protecting the environment are complex, and every decision made, whether as an individual, a company, a region, or a country, has a vast number of variables that interact with each other, sometimes unpredictably.

Take as an example the well-intentioned effort to convert American corn production, normally used for human consumption and animal feed, to produce ethanol, a clean-burning automobile fuel alternative that potentially could decrease U.S. dependence on foreign oil. The unexpected and inadvertent outcome was a global shortage of food and a sharp spike in the cost of corn-based food products. Moreover, the cost of producing the ethanol either is equal to or exceeds the price for which it is sold due to the high cost of production and use of fossil fuels to harvest it! Other issues such as conservation of lands for wildlife, impacts on human health, depletion of water tables, and destruction of old-growth and rain forests are all being widely contested for the betterment of the communities of people these systems support. Now that environmental sustainability is becoming mainstream (could this mean profitable?), unlikely alliances are forming all over the world between adversaries from the environmentalist community and the business community to achieve mutual goals. These public/private partnerships are now a critical success factor in any sustainability strategy.

Though the environmental issues require complex decisions that have positive and negative implications, there is no excuse for refusing to reflect on the implications and taking decisive action to change our behavior. William McDonough and Michael Braungart, authors of *Cradle to Cradle*, call for an end to creating products that are merely not bad or less harmful to the environment.[1] We need to create products that are essentially good in the first place. They propose reevaluating every product currently on the market, reducing each to its most essential composition and replacing components with an entirely new design that is not harmful to environment from its inception to its grave or to a reusable state. Companies that accomplish this can be certified Cradle to Cradle, and I believe this to be a clarion call for entrepreneurs, chemists, and designers to begin discovery. Others will pick up the gauntlet laid down by Fred Krupp in *Earth: The Sequel* and uncover the new energy sources and technologies for the burgeoning post-oil economy. For most companies, the beginning steps of reflecting on the issues and the changes they can make at the level they can successfully implement and maintain is a good start; and as they gain experience and increase awareness, more significant environmental impacts will emerge.

THE GREATER GREEN: SOCIAL EQUITY

What does social equity have to do with environmental sustainability? For some business owners, there is still a question about why this element of supporting a just and equitable society is a key component of an initiative to reduce the effects of climate change. Others who agree with keeping social equity as one of three outcomes of the triple bottom line can't provide a compelling reason why; it just seems to make sense. It made perfect sense during the industrial age: Henry Ford was an early adopter of the concept of social equity in the United States by setting a goal to build cars so affordable, even his factory workers could afford them. Access to affordable automobiles was one of the key foundations of economic prosperity in the country at the time, and a brilliant corporate strategy. This premise of affordability and access has a basic flaw, however: With limited resources and rising demand today from emerging economies reaching a crisis level throughout the world, it's not possible to transfer Ford's vision of an automobile in every garage for six billion people! But social equity is now a critical success in today's world because each person is connected economically to everyone else, as was evidenced during my trip to Nigeria.

I had the opportunity to travel to sub-Saharan Africa on and off for three years, and the country that struck me as the most representative of the disparities in our world was Nigeria. I was headed for Port Harcourt in the summer of 2005 for deploying e-learning systems in hospitals to train health-care practitioners in how to treat HIV/AIDS more effectively. I read that nearly 11 percent of U.S. oil is extracted from the region onshore and offshore of Port Harcourt and that it is a particularly rich form of crude—highly valuable. Revenues to Nigeria are in the billions of dollars annually, so I assumed Port Harcourt must be a paradise, being the oil port of call. Not so. Upon arrival at the airport, I was assaulted by the thick, acrid air and I was gasping for breath. Most of the ride into town passed through an enormous urban village with no pavement or sewage. The center of town was clogged with cars and had very few hotels to stay in. At night, the sky was a deep red, lit by the oil-burning flames from the pumps surrounding the city. I learned that the coastline and most of the rivers in the delta region were spoiled by oil spills over the past 30 years. I was shocked, and wondered how billions of dollars could flow through this community while very little seemed to have remained. Shortly after I left, several oil rigs were attacked by local rebels, and foreign oil workers were kidnapped for ransom; the rebels demanded compensation and a share of the oil profits. It is estimated that during the period of 2006 to 2008, the price of gasoline was affected on average by as much as $0.75 per gallon in the United States. Every violent attack, whether in Nigeria or elsewhere, would spur the price of oil upward. Think of it like this: We are like a big, global bowl of Jell-O and no matter where you are, if someone jiggles it, you're going to feel it.

The social equity issue is inextricably tied to the efforts and outcomes of sustainability. The community of Port Harcourt, Nigeria, is a living reminder that focusing on profits alone is not enough to ensure the betterment of life for all citizens. There is no trickle-down effect when it comes to social equity; it's a conscious effort based on basic human values of equality, equity, and long-term sustainability of the community. An important shift from the industrial age to the sustainability age, which we are rapidly approaching, is the role of the rich person moving toward the sustainable person. Rich people see themselves as rising above the masses to achieve their goals, and through their efforts the masses will benefit. But carelessness and unconscious (or conscious) disregard for the economic development of the community leads to careless destruction of the environment. Sustainable people have an element of caring about what happens in the community from the outset; they see their own success in relation to the success of the whole. This is not to say there will be no differences in compensation and rewards for hard work and innovation, but the attitude and behavior of the sustainable person will be that doing good is good for business.

MAKING GREEN: PROFITABILITY AND PERFORMANCE

Making a profit while going green sounds like a conflict of interest. How is it possible that you can continually grow a company and make a profit while the principle of sustainability (i.e., not taking more than you need or replacing what you've taken) seems to contradict it? The answer to this seeming conundrum is voiced by Einstein when he stated, "No problem can be solved from the same level of consciousness that created it." Innovation and enterprise have a fundamental principle at work: If there is a market, a product will meet the demand, even when resources are diminishing and demand for products is increasing. At the 2007 GreenBuild Conference in Chicago, facilities managers and their C-level superiors were disappointed in the dearth of products available created to meet the new sustainability demands for their administration buildings and production facilities. They came in larger numbers that year with checks in hand to buy green. "We don't want a particleboard conference table made of recycled wood for our executive boardroom," complained one facilities executive. "We want green, sustainable materials with great design at an affordable price." Innovative entrepreneurs will fill the demand. Now more companies are buying sustainable fabrics, carpets, paints, and other materials because a few manufacturers took the risk to meet the rising demand.

The profitable roofing company at the facilities forum described its new definition of a roof on behalf of customers as a garden, an energy collector through solar and wind, a heat deflector, a protector from the elements, an exercise area, a stargazing platform, a rain collector, and a beautiful design element of the home. The company suggests cost savings to the purchaser as energy savings, a cooler/warmer building, water savings, increased value of the home, and energy tax credits. A green housing developer surveyed his customers and found that among all of the green innovations available in a home, such as efficiency, quality, and low impact on the environment, the greatest need was for a home to promote human health. His profitable housing development is now measuring the changes of tenant health before and after moving in.

Profitability and performance of a business or organization are intrinsic to success in sustainability and not inherently contradictory because of increasing global population and more demands for an American lifestyle. Rather, in the demands from the Green Rush, innovations are redefining our materials, our delivery systems, our use, and even our wants for products in more sustainable ways. Obviously, consumer demand can be manipulated through clever marketing, but that mentality, through economics and necessity, is changing. Our wants and needs as consumers will need to adapt and conform to increasing costs from diminishing resources and narrowing of profit margins.

During the early stages of adopting sustainability practices, most companies will experience a loss. It costs more to go green. Just go to a whole foods store or co-op grocery and look for local, fair-trade, and organic products and you will see a 20 to 50 percent higher price compared to traditional counterparts. For many consumers, this price discrepancy is outweighed by their vision of green, social equity, and the health of their family. But not everyone can afford these products. It's going to take longer, and the marketplace has to grow enough that prices become lower so that demand increases. The trend is moving toward green as more and more traditionally produced products are either being pulled from the shelves or being re-created to meet the rising demand. Once cost savings are realized, the entrepreneur needs to create value beyond efficient, low-cost production and distribution. The product must provide differentiation from others similarly labeled. Long-term profitability and growth for sustainable products is no different than for other products from an earlier industrial age: The organization must be run well and products must be high-quality, be cost-effective, meet consumer expectations, and incorporate a good design. Nor should we forget the contributions of the intrepid investor; they too are motivated by profit and can also find meaning and profit in new ways.

Another dimension about profitability is wealth. One of the most challenging books I read in my own odyssey of learning more about the trends of the sustainability age was *Good News for a Change* by David Suzuki and Holly Dressel.[2] The book described not only how companies were struggling to innovate and thrive while changing their businesses to be more sustainable, but also how these entrepreneurs made personal changes toward wealth. Some of these business owners realigned themselves with the concept of wealth to include time with family, connection to the community, meaning and purpose in their everyday actions, and time for thoughtful, intentioned reflection on how they can make the world a better place for others. Many of the wealthiest Americans such as Bill Gates are leaving their positions and applying their time and wealth for philanthropy, so there is no argument for becoming wealthy. What is challenging about this realignment towards wealth is the implication that we must consider the option of living with less. Not everyone will be able to live the traditional middle-class lifestyle of the United States, but we still need to address the desire of the rest of the world to emulate this lifestyle. It's actually overconsumption that needs to be addressed, even in the context of consumers desiring to go green: I recently heard someone mention that they had bought three new Priuses as an effort to use less fuel! Others may be building a new completely green home, but it is a 10,000-square-foot house on newly developed land.

The American economy has the opportunity to lead this change through its unparalleled tradition of solving problems against seemingly insurmountable odds, finding a way to meet new demands, and sustaining an enterprise through difficult times through adaptation and creativity. The world watches what the United States does. It is a great incubator for ideas and creator of lifestyles that everyone wants to emulate. I'm always inspired by the scene in the movie *Apollo 13* in which a group of engineers, cloistered in a room with identical materials as in the distressed space module, are told they have limited time to create a breathing apparatus with incompatible parts and write a simple procedure that can be followed by the astronauts. Go!

SMART GREEN VERSUS GREENWASHING

Developing an effective strategy requires foresight, reflection, and careful planning. In regard to sustainability, misfiring on your strategy and your message to the public, especially your clients, can have catastrophic effects. As many companies leap into the Green Rush without taking the time to carefully craft their strategies and their marketing messages, their customers, who have become savvy to greenwashing, will easily recognize the signs. An obvious example of this is when companies use the word or color green with their product with no proof of sustainable activity to back it up. While intent to go green is commendable, it's not a good idea to broadcast the change before it has actually happened. An important aspect of the Smart Green company is the concept of planning a strategy with a clear mission toward sustainability at the level you can implement, have incremental growth in stages, and achieve measurable results. The contrary view to this strategic planning approach is the greenwashing company. To illustrate this concept of the Smart Green versus greenwashing more clearly, Table 3.1 outlines the differences in direction that companies take on the journey toward being successful and sustainable.

A Smart Green company takes the time to plan its strategy for sustainability in small increments and build upon the successes of measurable results. As the results indicate a positive return on a small scale, that effort can either help to fund other efforts or be rolled out across the enterprise for a greater return on investment (ROI). A greenwashing company would prefer to act swiftly with an initiative without thinking through all of the issues or implications of

Table 3.1   Strategic Planning Differences between Smart Green vs.
Greenwashing Companies

Smart Green Company	Greenwashing Company
Strategic planning at the level of ability to implement	Act now, plan later
Measurement of outcomes	Spray and Pray
Transparency	Controlled marketing messages
Systems view for broader community, world	Self-preservation
Incremental, long-term growth	Fast growth with short-term financial gains
Outcomes based on Triple bottom-line	Financial bottom-line only

that decision. Perhaps that company is worried about rising competition jumping on the sustainability bandwagon and its own actions appearing to reflect a me-too mentality. The long-term effect is harmful not only to the company leaping before thinking, but also to the community of individuals and organizations working toward sustainable practices that may be lumped into the so-called green fatigue that is now seemingly plaguing consumers. Everything starts looking the same with little or no distinction when there are actually significant differences. An interesting note about disclosure of sustainability activities is that many companies in Europe have been silently developing sustainable practices for many years and have consciously decided not to disclose their activities until required to do so as part of a regional effort to increase transparency of sustainable corporations.

Because Smart Green companies implement their strategies with a means to measure their outcomes both financially and non-financially, they are able to calibrate their efforts more effectively for the best results. A fact sheet released by the Clinton Climate Initiative in Chicago, Illinois describes its C40 Large Cities Climate Leadership Group in the context of measuring outcomes: "To enable partner cities to reduce energy use and greenhouse gas emissions,

CCI is: Creating a purchasing consortium to pool the buying power of cities in order to lower the prices of energy-efficient products and to accelerate the development of new energy-saving technologies. . . . Mobilizing the best technical experts in the world and creating local capacity to develop and implement programs that result in reduced energy use and greenhouse gas emissions. . . . Developing common measurement and information flow tools that allow cities to track the effectiveness of their programs and share what works and does not work with each other."

Greenwashing companies implement their projects with little or no effort to measure their outcomes, a kind of "spray and pray" method of implementation with the hope that if they give a generalized message or change their Web site to include children, grass, and mountains (with no real changes in the products or services), someone will buy from them. Spray and pray is expensive in the long run because without measurable, assignable results, the marketing message, product, service, and image portrayed will not sustain the diversity of interests and the scrutiny of well-informed customers.

A Smart Green company looks at its strategy as part of an overall system, connected to its community and ultimately to the world. The implication: Changes in a company's carbon footprint (levels of greenhouse gases such as carbon dioxide emitted into the atmosphere) are just the beginning. Each company has suppliers, shippers, vendors, growers, extractors, and/or manufacturers that contribute to the overall footprint of the enterprise. One change in the daisy chain of product supply begins the process of change for all members of the product life cycle. Bradley Yoder of Triangle PolySteel is seeking to make an impact on the sustainability of such a system, but he realizes it's still early: "I'm just a one-man show at this time and no not have much clout. Most vendors are in an efficiency mindset and not necessarily one of sustainability. They haven't changed their procedures or methods or products much yet. Though customers really like the idea of a sustainable product or system, not as many of them as I'd like are putting their money into it. Some are sold on the idea and understand the value, and that is the way they are going. We as a society are not sold yet on the whole systems approach to sustainability. It sometimes takes a lot of time and energy to communicate to consumers the value of choosing products based on their sustainability. It's not a quick sell, yet. I see my role as helping to shift the market to a new mindset so that 'thinking green' and 'buying green' become second nature. Imagine how different the world would look if we truly did that?"

A Smart Green company develops its strategy with the intent of affecting the larger issue of its carbon footprint, whereas a greenwashing company is more interested and concerned about self-preservation and will say what it needs to say to get a customer, retain a customer, or buy from any vendor or supplier without regard to a greater sustainability strategy. Moreover, a Smart Green company will carefully consider the outcomes of its strategy in terms of the triple bottom line of sustainability (which includes environmental stewardship), social equity, and profitability and performance. Results from this approach will take the form of different types of metrics, not all of them financial, and they can indicate a return on investment in appropriate terms for each aspect of the triple bottom line. Nancy Murray, executive director of Builders of Hope in Raleigh, North Carolina, brings the triple bottom line into focus in her strategy by starting with homes slated for demolition and headed to the landfill. She utilizes a neglected workforce to retrofit the homes in a new location and creates new, affordable homes that are energy-efficient. "Our process of building affordable housing provides environmental, social and economic solutions to the local communities where we build through the recycling of unwanted homes and re-using 80% or more of the original structure—saving millions of pounds of debris from the landfill—retrofitting of green building standards, integration of energy efficiencies using Advanced Energy's System Vision Program, and the re-training and employment of the homeless and at-risk youth to fill the on-site construction labor positions through our work mentor program. The process starts out with a donated home and the economies of taking a free structure allows for generous enough margins to rehab 'green' and still sell the house for below its appraised value."

Greenwashing companies will usually ignore the first two aspects—people and planet—and have a stronger focus on short-term gains for profit. If these companies don't take the time to draw conclusions about the effects of their actions and become aware of the social, economic, and environmental statistics of their region, none of the outcomes of the triple bottom line are going to matter, including profitability. All of these aspects are interconnected, and each has long-term implications for all organizations. By analyzing yourself in the context of the differences between Smart Green and greenwashing, it becomes clear what stage of change you may be in. Smart Green companies are in the stages of action and maintenance, whereas most greenwashing companies are contemplating sustainability and taking action prematurely.

Another important strategic planning strategy is to determine your level of greenth—that level at which your company can adequately implement and sustain change toward becoming sustainable.

WHAT IS YOUR LEVEL OF GREENTH?

Before you can embark on your strategic plan and launch a project, you need to be very clear about the level of awareness and ability to implement that your organization can sustain. Oftentimes, an individual with a vision to have zero emissions or have a product developed with completely natural processes and materials is out of sync with what is possible today and who can provide buy-in, support, and materials at the level the individual can implement. At a recent conference on regionalism, growth, and sustainability, over 100 regional planners and organizers shared their projects with each other over several days. Some metropolitan areas, like Portland, Oregon, have already met the emissions requirements of the Kyoto Protocol (which the United States has not yet adopted), while other metropolitan areas, such as Salt Lake City, are just getting started with obtaining buy-in from the community for an emissions-reduction plan by introducing light rail for the first time. The participants in both regions share the same passion for the same goal but are at different ends of the spectrum in the types of actions they can take, given their respective communities. Portland is ready to go beyond the Kyoto Protocol, and Salt Lake City is ready to begin planning its growth beyond the normal 20-year period to a 50-year plan. According to their awareness and ability to act on sustainability initiatives, these two communities are at different levels of greenth. Individuals, organizations, communities, regions, and countries can all have varied levels of greenth intermingled with each other; however, the intended project must be calibrated to the correct level of greenth of the organization and its constituents (stakeholders, staff, customers, suppliers) for there to be success.

There is no certification for levels of greenth; these levels are highly subjective and based on perceptions of one's own and others' practices. Official certifications such as Leadership in Energy and Environmental Design (LEED) or Green Seal or Cradle to Cradle help provide a shorthand description of the company's actions, but levels of greenth are not dependent on or defined by these certifications. It is generally possible to implement a successful sustainability initiative with those at the same level of greenth or immediately lower than you are, but more difficult to work with those that are at higher levels. Table 3.2 is an example of a simple spectrum of levels of greenth. Each level is given a tree-related name to keep an environmental theme present. There are many more criteria to consider for the levels than this simplified model, but it illustrates the concept.

The spectrum of greenth presented in the chart is divided into four levels to illustrate an ever-increasing level of awareness and complexity of actions. On the left side are sample categories of awareness and action that an organization can take, and the columns to the right reveal how they progress through each level. This chart is by no means comprehensive or definitive, but it illustrates the importance of matching, at a rudimentary level, your level of greenth with your sustainability strategy. It briefly describes possible contributions an organization makes or is aware of for each category at each level.

Greenth Level 1

The most basic of the levels of greenth in practice starts with the most fundamental changes toward sustainability, such as providing a healthy and safe working environment; switching to nontoxic cleaning materials; providing a living wage or higher for employees; implementing a reduce, recycle, reuse program for all employees and

Table 3.2   Levels of Greenth: Complete Columns Depending on Your Region

Sample Company Activities	Level I	Level II	Level III	Level IV
Organizational Structure				
Employee Relations				
Strategic Plan				
Carbon Footprint				
Transparency				
Community Service				
Water Usage				
Product Life cycle				
Measurement Approach				
Certification				
Marketing				
Transportation				
Energy				
Custom Activity				
Custom Activity				

facilities; providing educational programs on energy efficiency for all employees; increasing diversity in hiring practices; introducing the LEED Bronze certification for all facilities; practicing basic waste and water management changes; and purchasing from vendors practicing recycling. There are no significant changes to products except recycled packaging and reduced energy and fuel for shipping and handling. Marketing a Level 1 company is limited to labeling paper and other goods as recycled, hiring practices for diversity of staff, and commitment to progressing toward more sustainable practices.

Greenth Level 2

At this level, inclusive of the Greenth Level 1, the Level 2 has progressed to having all of its packaging, paper goods, and other similar items come from 100 percent recycled sources. Diversity of staff is represented by age, gender, race, and so on. Benefits for employees may include health care, a pension or 401(k) plan, and bonuses. Additionally, the Level 2 company may have introduced flextime and working from home, and emphasizes the importance of working normal hours to have more time with family. Furthermore, at least one facility is seeking LEED Silver certification, and considerations for changing the processes and components of products to be less harmful to the environment and for the health of workers are being discussed. Many more efforts to decrease energy and oil consumption and to diversify energy sources are under way. Marketing the Twig company includes more transparency of its energy consumption, and commitment to sustainable practices within its facilities. Its sustainability mission is more prominently presented on printed materials, on its Web site, and as part of new employee orientation.

Greenth Level 3

At this level, the Greenth Level 3 company is inclusive of the previous levels and is now actively redesigning its production, distribution, delivery, use, and waste of its processes and products. More employee involvement in strategic management decisions is evident. The Level 3 company may invest in more certification programs to demonstrate its commitment to sustainable practices such as the Global Reporting Initiative (GRI) for greater transparency of its practices and emissions, Green Seal certification for its products and processes, and LEED Gold for its facilities. The Branch company establishes higher goals for emissions reduction and product development that has zero impact from its creation to waste within a shorter time frame. Marketing the products of the Branch company is more direct, and their green status as a differentiator over competitors' products is highly visible to the public, customers, vendors, investors, and other stakeholders.

Greenth Level 4

At this level, the Green Level 4 company is practicing the highest form possible of sustainable practices given the current technology.

Its energy sources are off the grid that uses petroleum- or nuclear-based sources, it has zero emissions, and its products are all produced and certified as Cradle to Cradle—there is no impact on the environment from extraction to waste in its product life cycle. Tree companies may be worker-owned with a strong commitment to development of the broader community. All stakeholders in the Tree company are less concerned with certifications and more interested in maintaining its sustainable production while also being a strong community advocate and being profitable. Marketing the Level 4 company is based on the company's reputation and benefit to customers as having products that are created without harm to the environment and are reusable or recyclable at the time they are to be thrown out.

The levels of greenth illustrated here are a suggested basic guide for you as an entrepreneur to determine where you land in your ability to implement sustainability initiatives successfully without a mismatch internally with your stakeholders and externally to the community at large. A significant aspect of determining your level of greenth is to explore your definition of sustainability, the next step in your journey toward developing a sustainability strategy. How you define sustainability guides your strategic planning process and leads to the next step: a sustainability needs analysis.

ANALYSIS OF YOUR CORPORATE BIOSPHERE

A needs analysis is an opportunity for you to revisit the research you have conducted on the community in which you reside and conduct business. There are essentially four dimensions of the needs analysis that relate specifically to your sustainability strategic plan that Smart Green companies utilize: footprint analysis, product life cycle analysis, business relationship analysis, and cash flow analysis. A useful beginning tool is a sustainability assessment form. Traditional forms of sustainability analyses are conducted for fulfilling certification purposes and present a description of impacts on elements of the triple bottom line: social equity, profitability, and environmental stewardship. Most of these checklists are either specific to a particular industry or generic and less adaptable to various types and sizes of companies.

Since the goal of the certification process is to inspire meaningful change toward having less of an impact on the environment, more consideration needs to be made to helping companies contextualize the activities within their local environment and relationships within the community, demonstrate the value financially, and collect data to prove positive impact on a periodic basis. Sample assessments can be accessed through some chambers of commerce or accessible online. For example, The Institute for Sustainable Development, Green Plus™, a tool and a process designed to educate small businesses about sustainable business policies and practices and to reward top performers with certification. Green Plus is also a social networking platform with wiki functionality where business owners and managers interested in going green and sustainable can share best practices, source good actionable information, and interact with and learn from their peers from across the country.[3]

The first of four dimensions to explore for the sustainability needs assessment is your footprint analysis.

Footprint Analysis

As Figure 3.1 indicates, placing your business at the center of a flow of product, the footprint analysis determines the current impact your business is having on each aspect of the environmental system that includes water, air, land, energy, transportation, waste, and so on, as well as the economical and social systems in the community. For example, a landscaping company has equipment, trucks, chemicals, and fertilizers to run its business. It purchases supplies, equipment, plants, maintenance services, and fuel from area businesses. It delivers these services to clients and businesses within its delivery region. It disposes of waste in the form of plant debris, paper, plastic, chemicals, and construction materials at the landfill. It directly or indirectly is dependent upon water to ensure success of its projects. It uses equipment to conduct the service that burns fuel and emits a lot of noise. Rather than measuring the impact of one business alone, the

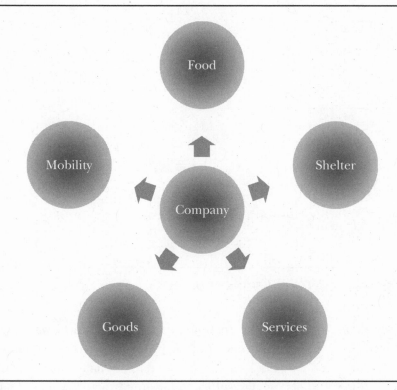

Figure 3.1   The Footprint Analysis includes some of the impacts the company alone has on the environment.

entire system must be analyzed. This system is reinforced by suppliers providing cost-effective and convenient access to products and services as well as customers willing to buy the service in its present form, until there is a change of perception within this system. Direct and indirect impacts need to be determined for each aspect of the system on the environment and community.

The second dimension to explore for the sustainability needs assessment is the product life cycle analysis.

Product Life Cycle Analysis

Placing your business at the center of a flow of product, the product life cycle analysis determines the pathway of your product from the point of extraction to its manufacture, distribution, retail, delivery, use, and waste (see Figure 3.2). At each stage of the product life cycle, to the best

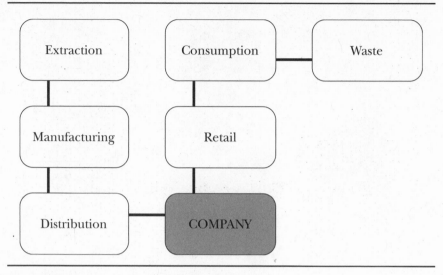

Figure 3.2   Product Life Cycle Analysis

of your ability, determine the amount of energy, by-products, waste, and costs associated with the movement of the product from one stage to the next. Though you may not be able to have an immediate effect on those vendors and suppliers initially, sufficient pressure from a number of buyers will change their behavior. Vance Remick of the General Store Café wanted to buy local eggs and not those from a regional supplier whose eggs were not as fresh, whose chickens were not treated humanely, and whose refrigerated trucks burned a lot of fuel. By working through a local agricultural cooperative to provide leverage, the local egg providers were able to obtain certifications from the state agricultural inspector, whose office was in the larger egg producer's location!

The third dimension to explore for the sustainability needs assessment is the business relationship analysis.

Business Relationship Analysis

Placing your business at the center of a flow of product, the business relationship analysis (see Figure 3.3) determines the current impact your business is having on each of the contributors and recipients of your system to appreciate, understand, and improve the quality of these relationships for expanding the circle of the sustainability impact. For example, the landscaping company maintains a close relationship

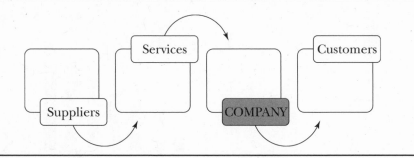

Figure 3.3 Business Relationship Analysis illustrates the transactional agreement that exist to benefit the company that may or may not be beneficial to the environment nor the community.

with its clients to ensure on-time, cost-effective, quality service. For vendors, the company maintains a relationship for credit accounts, bulk purchases, availability of product, and convenience. This social network will change when the vision of the company changes either to adapt to customer requests (marketing response) or to fulfill a vision to reduce environmental impact (personal change response). A decision to change even one element of the system, such as refusing to use pesticides and instead using a nontoxic alternative, will potentially increase labor costs, may increase costs to the customer, and may require changing vendors. The customer and the vendor are impacted directly financially but they are also challenged to understand the company's decision and to make a decision for themselves. Education across the entire system is critical if there is one participant deciding to change.

The fourth dimension to explore for the sustainability needs assessment is the cash flow analysis.

The Cash Flow Analysis

Creating a cash flow analysis (Figure 3.4) and determining return on investment for systemic change are critical before embarking on a sustainability strategy. Investment into sustainability can be considered to be in the same category as innovative research because in some ways many of the financial outcomes are unknown, but the possible growth of business is imminent if you innovate early and effectively. Depending on the business and the level of change required throughout the company's systems, the cost is likely to be greater than it would

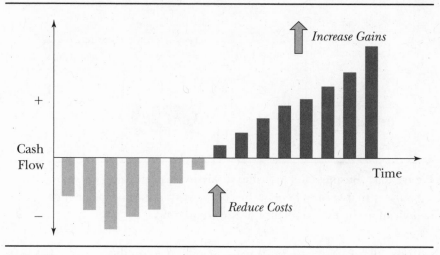

Figure 3.4   The Cash Flow Analysis illustrates the business case for the payback period and return on investment of sustainability initiatives.

be when maintaining current levels of operation. To mitigate the risk, the business case can guide the company through each element of the investment, its potential benefits and risks, costs, and short- and long-term financial impact. With the system and relationship analysis much of the risk can be avoided. The extra cost of the change can possibly be offset with increase of new business, rebates and government subsidies, or other creative solutions. A landscaping company may ask customers to buy sustainability credits to help fund the change for next year's service—like an organic farm cooperative.

Measurement of outcomes needs to reflect impacts on each element of the triple bottom line to maintain the efficiency and effectiveness of the system, product life cycle, business relationships, and the business case. Once you have collected this important information, you are ready to begin the strategic planning process by writing a Smart Green mission statement.

WRITING A SMART GREEN MISSION STATEMENT

The final stage of preparing to develop a sustainability strategic plan is to write a mission statement, including goals and objectives; define the desired outcomes; and nurture stakeholder support. This stage is extremely important because it represents the first chance you have of writing down your assumptions, beliefs, and conclusions about all that you have learned, and apply them to a plan of action. You will likely be giving a PowerPoint presentation of your ideas until you're blue in the face. Just realize you can't do it alone. You have employees, customers, vendors, suppliers, partners, investors, bankers, and even spouses or other family members who need to see clearly what you are seeing. The plan may need to be tempered to adapt to a common, achievable goal once you have gone through this process of sharing your ideas with others.

The first step in defining your mission is to outline your beliefs and assumptions about your company, its purpose, and its value proposition in relation to the three aspects of the triple bottom line. In many ways, writing a mission statement for your strategy is like writing an elevator pitch. For example, if your project is to begin a recycling campaign for the company, your elevator speech may be: "A recycling campaign for our company will enable all of our employees to work together in a common purpose to recycle or reuse products not only for cost savings of up to 45 percent but also to reduce our environmental impact of adding to the landfill." In this single sentence, you have shared a component of people working toward a common goal (social aspect), reducing waste in the landfill (planet), and saving the company money (profit). And just like an elevator pitch, the key to a successful mission statement is that it must be succinct. In one or two sentences, it must describe your strategy and provide a budget amount and believable financial and nonfinancial benefits to each aspect of the triple bottom line.

The next step is to expand your mission statement to be more specific about goals, objectives, tasks, and a budget to prepare for your presentation. This can take the form of an executive summary of your overall strategic plan to gain initial support and buy-in from key stakeholders, particularly funders, to proceed with the planning process, implementation, and analysis. The executive summary should be no more than one page and should share your mission, the goal of the project, the basic approach you are using, the budget, and the expected outcomes and benefits. For example, a computer software and consulting firm wanted to justify investment into the development of a cloud computing center that would benefit students and faculty from high schools, community colleges, and universities across the state. Here is the executive summary:

> Acme Software Company seeks $1.2M for the development and deployment of the XYZ Cloud Computing Center and to demonstrate optimal sustainability for the cloud computing deployment. The project will add additional, energy-efficient blade servers to a preexisting bank of servers and will be developed with open source code in partnership with eight participating software providers, each agreeing to provide access to their products free of charge to students and faculty in the state and on a micro-fee basis for all other users. The cloud computing project serves the purpose of providing high-quality, state-of-the-art research tools to the most remote and economically challenged regions of the state without the high cost of computers, facilities, and licenses to the software normally incurred on campuses.

> This approach not only saves the state money; it also increases the workforce and research capacity of the state to attract investment and encourage companies to move here. Moreover, with no facilities to build, the cost of building and maintaining new facilities is avoided and energy costs and impacts on the environment are reduced. Moreover, the servers and the facilities used to house them are utilizing state-of-the-art techniques to reduce carbon emissions and increase energy efficiency. The cloud computing center can accommodate tens of thousands of simultaneous users at a fraction of the cost (which would be unapproachable) of scaling up individual computer centers on campuses.

Notice the outcomes defined in terms of the triple bottom line. As more agencies, funders, investors, and other stakeholders become aware and informed about sustainability, these outcomes will become more and more expected. An executive summary can then be translated into other forms for presentation, such as a PowerPoint slide presentation, a Flash media presentation online, or a YouTube video.

The next step is presenting to stakeholders. My experience has been to share only the "need to know" information, but be prepared to answer a lot of questions. First, identify who the key stakeholders are. Who is the decision maker, who is someone who can influence the decision maker, and who is going to have the responsibility to make sure you complete the project on time and within budget? During the presentation, embed your vision and outcomes for sustainability as if they are inextricably linked to the main purposes the stakeholders are interested in: profitability and ROI. You can't prove these things yet. Define the parameters of your project, including technical and organizational requirements, costs, time frame for planning and implementation, and contributors to the project. Define the desired sustainability outcomes. What problem is this deployment going to solve? Whose interests are being served? What are the expected outcomes from immediate key stakeholders in the project? Once you have shared each of the elements of your project through the executive summary and have answered all the questions that you can, you'll most likely be given the go-ahead to develop your strategic plan, implementation, and measurement process.

"I appreciate what you saved the company last quarter, but what have you done for me lately?" This refrain can be heard in every type of organization around the country. What's actually being asked is, "I just want you to cut costs on a regular basis, and I don't care how you do it." Leaders realize that there is potentially a lack of alignment between the roles of their contribution to the organization as perceived by upper management or their internal clients and how they communicate their contribution to the bottom line of the company. Strategy for an organization conjures up all the mission statements and vision phrases used to provide guidance and direction for management, departments, teams, and individuals. Most experts agree that organizational success is largely dependent upon how well and how clearly employees are aligned with the stated strategy. Establishing and implementing a strategic plan proves to be one of the most difficult activities leaders in organizations experience. As a result, organizations spend millions of dollars annually to achieve this balance of a clearly defined strategy, coherence of the strategy across the enterprise, and an effective coordination plan. Over the wide spectrum of strategy development processes and services, none are more elusive and difficult to harness than the Smart Green strategic planning process. Within this process, the most important success factors are measurement of the outcomes—the financial and non-financial benefits of sustainability realized by the investment and strategy alignment—and the degree by which employees feel they own the strategy, which is in direct correlation to the success of the strategy as a whole—with elements of ownership, commitment, and involvement in the vision.

4

Smart Green
Strategic Planning

When you innovate, you've got to be prepared for
everyone telling you you're nuts.

—*Larry Ellison*

STRATEGIC PLANNING AND SUSTAINABILITY

Smart Green companies are driven by results. The vision of sustainability, however you wish to define it, will be maintained and grow in complexity as long as there is a clear plan, measurable outcomes for each aspect of the triple bottom line, and support from stakeholders. Whether you are an entrepreneur running your own company or an internal manager responsible for lines of business within an organization, the principles of developing a strategic plan should concentrate on the ideals of sustainability and the ability to be profitable. Meanwhile, managers and entrepreneurs are also increasingly concerned with making sure their sustainability strategy is authentic and acceptable as representative of the triple bottom line as perceived by stakeholders, employees, and customers. The negative effects of greenwashing—marketing your sustainability efforts above and beyond your actual efforts—must be avoided at all costs. The benefits of taking it slow, planning carefully according to the level of greenth among all stakeholders, and justifying the costs with business results will far outweight a quick solution to compete with an increasingly green competitor.

In *The Strategy-Led Business*, Kerry Napuk explains that a company's strategic plan is "a total concept of the whole business involving a framework and process that guides its future."[1] For many companies, a strategic plan takes the lowest form of a project plan and establishes a goal, objectives, tasks, and budget. With the new dimensions introduced by sustainability, a Smart Green company has to go beyond the traditional project planning mode and consider more variables. Moreover, the ability to weather the storm of differences of opinion, stops and starts of new projects, long-term results, and new metrics associated with the triple bottom line demands a more comprehensive strategic plan—in the form of a business case for internal managers and a business plan for entrepreneurs starting a new company.

A sustainability strategic plan must be inclusive of information normally found in a business case, because all of the motivations and actions need to be tested and evaluated against the rigors of financial justification. Otherwise, all good intentions aside, the business will flounder from lack of understanding of the business drivers of actions. "It's an economic market that is going to continue to grow forever," says Tom VanZeeland of RainEscape™, which provides rain catchment technology, Aquaeras™, for homes and business, describing the motivations behind his strategic plan. "We've turned a corner in the building process and the economic market to where the consumers are looking at the impact rather than just getting the bare minimum price."

For Smart Green companies to proceed with an effective sustainability strategic plan, they need to step out of the traditional planning mode and tap into new perspectives and new tools that stretch their assumptions and expectations beyond where they have ever been before. More is at stake and therefore more is expected: a new strategic planning framework that incorporates these seemingly contradictory aspirations of sustainability and commercial enterprise. The best of both worlds coming together, involving new relationships and alliances not considered possible before, can culminate in a win-win for the planet and people with new levels of creativity, innovation, growth, and meaning.

FOOTPRINTS IN THE SAND

Like the organic basis for life, the unfolding of your strategic plan resembles the interrelations between molecules, cells, and organisms growing and living within a dynamic biosphere. As the conditions of the biosphere change, each organic element and life form subsequently either adapts and thrives or ignores the changing conditions and perishes. Each organic element is inextricably linked to others that grow from one connection to quantum levels of connection—a web of life. Two principles of nature encourage the growth and complexity of this web of life. The first is that small changes in a few individual life forms that adapt well to environmental change lead change throughout the entire web. The second is that new connections are made where there is an opportunity to grow and a gap in the web. So what does all this mean for your strategic plan? These principles in nature are like footprints in the sand, and all you have to do is follow them.

First, imagine a company that has a building, property, staff, and its product (see Figure 4.1). This company utilizes resources to operate, produce, and sell its product, and has an environmental impact on its particular community—known as its environmental footprint. This footprint is characterized by the annual sum total of carbon emissions it releases into the atmosphere, water use and disposal, all other forms of waste, land usage, effects on flora and fauna, and effects on human health.

In this image, the company is surrounded by its footprint emissions and other effects, represented by a gray halo. The circular area is the community where the company resides. Now imagine this company with its own footprint, but connected to the company

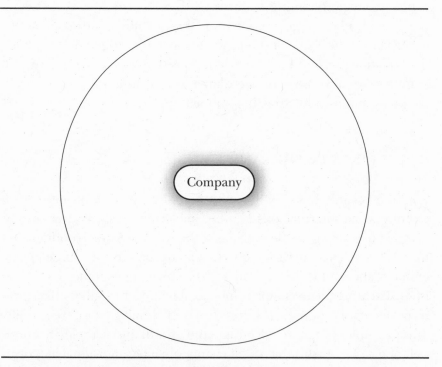

Figure 4.1   The Company Footprint

are its partners, vendors, and professional support (see Figure 4.2). Each of these connections has a building, property, staff, and its own product. Customers are also connected to the company with a smaller footprint individually, but as a community of consumers, they represent a very large footprint. Like the individual company in Figure 4.1, all of the other types of companies utilize resources to operate, produce, and sell their products and services and have a cumulative environmental impact on the community.

In this diagram, not only does the company have its own footprint, but it's also part of a larger sphere of influence represented as the direct relationships with its customers, alliance partners, vendors, and professional service providers. Each of these direct relationships also has its own footprint and in addition contributes to the collective footprint as part of its relationship to the company, thereby having an impact on the community.

Beyond the company's customers, partners, vendors, and professional service providers, the company has indirect relationships

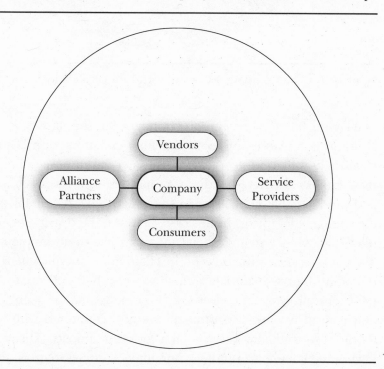

Figure 4.2   The Company Footprint with Direct Relationships

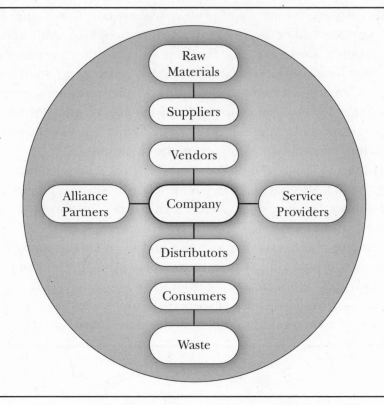

Figure 4.3   The Company Footprint with Indirect Relationships

(see Figure 4.3). On one end, the company has suppliers of raw materials for its goods and services. At the other end, it has distributors of the product, as well as waste after the customer has disposed of it. Many of these entities also have buildings, properties, vehicles, machinery, staff, and products that contribute to the overall environmental impact of the company footprint. In this case, however, the distributors and suppliers also service many other companies like the example company. They also represent the links of the chain in the product life cycle from the point the raw materials are extracted to their delivery to the company. This process can consume an enormous amount of energy, water, and natural resources. Customers are also connected with a smaller footprint individually, but in total a very large impact. The cumulative environmental impact on the community continues to grow.

In Figure 4.3, the company not only has its own footprint but it is also part of a larger sphere of influence represented by direct and indirect relationships with distributors, suppliers, and the disposal of its product by customers. The company purchases components of its product or the whole product from a vendor, which is receiving its components from a centralized supplier. Each of these relationships is maintained by a continuous flow of purchased products from companies as in this example. When customers eventually throw the company's product away, it may end up in a landfill, which contributes to an increasing problem of waste by-products, diminishing land use for waste, and toxicity from the product if it is burned or buried.

The relationships established within this greater footprint with the company at the center are repeated thousands of times within each industry sector. For example, in the agricultural sector, the grocery store chain represents the company; customers drive to the store for their food and other products and throw away the boxes, cans, and bottles; vendors provide the basic supplies for the grocery store to function, such as cash registers, grocery carts, paper goods, and storage shelves, and bring the food from regional centers; the professional service providers help the store with legal, accounting, and marketing services; and the suppliers are first the manufacturers and packagers of the food, and second the food growers themselves.

This sector-based ecosystem is repeated throughout the country and in the global economy as a web of influence (including transportation, retail, buildings and homes, communications, electronics, and so on) that fuels our economy and likewise has a tremendous impact on our environment. In Figure 4.4 this web stretches on and intersects with other sectors. In the industrial age, forming and maintaining integrity of this web has been the goal and measure of success.

Within each industry sector, a small number of suppliers and distributors may be at the center of the network, providing services to multiple companies. Each of these extended company footprints with an insatiable appetite for unlimited growth exponentially compounds the negative impacts on the environment. This strategic model is not sustainable in the long run with a growing population, diminishing resources, climate change, and the subsequent global warming. The role of the individual enterprise led by a visionary entrepreneur has now become critical. The changes that need to take place cannot be solved within the current structure humanity has created. It's simply not sustainable and that's bad for business.

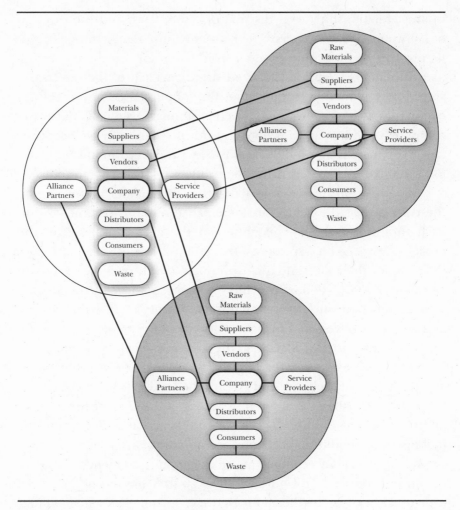

Figure 4.4   The Sector of Relationships

The radical idea is that every product, process, and relationship within the economic ecosystem needs to be re-created to be, as William McDonough has argued, "good," rather than "less bad" eventually. The push-back to this idea is cost, time, and know-how. Cost is not a reason for not developing alternative product designs, because new customers and investors are coming forward demanding a change, which creates a market opportunity. Time is also not a factor, because the clock is ticking on the depletion of resources, and alternatives are required anyway. Know-how should also not be an excuse, because entrepreneurs have been innovating new products and processes competitively for centuries.

Smart Green companies are aware of these forces and anticipate the changes by being clear about how changes in these sectors, caused by internal and external forces, affect business relationships, product life cycles, and profitability. In this case nature can help: In developing your sustainability strategic plan, two forces of change that occur in nature can be harnessed for your benefit to maximize your positive impact on the environment, social equity, and financial growth: adaptation and plasticity.

SUSTAINABLE STRATEGY 1: ADAPTATION

In nature, adaptation is the process by which significant, long-term external forces impact an organism or community of organisms, causing them to adjust to the changes or perish. These external forces could be atmospheric or geological, such as temperature change, earthquake, flood, fire, or volcano; they could be extraterrestrial, such as a large meteorite striking the earth or a comet trail passing through our atmosphere; or they could be biological, such as a new competitive species arriving in the area where one organism has had hegemony. Whatever outside forces are at work, organisms that adapt are the ones that survive and potentially thrive. Others, like the dinosaurs after what may have been an asteroid catastrophe, didn't survive in that form. Through a process of genetic mutation, many species develop new traits and abilities to survive despite changed circumstances. Think of woolly mammoths in the far north during the last ice age and their furless cousins in warmer Africa and India. This principle of adaptation applies to a Smart Green company's sustainability strategy that begins with awareness of new forces of change that consumers believe to be significant and timely for changing their buying habits. Some companies will greenwash their approach and attempt to cash in on the green hype, not realizing this change in consumers is not hype but a megatrend that is challenging our current assumptions about our global economy.

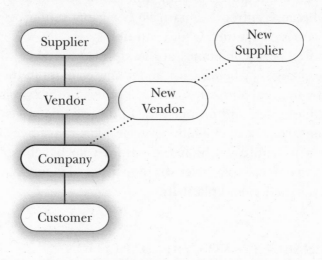

Figure 4.5   Adaptation

Figure 4.5 illustrates how customers begin to reduce certain kinds of consumption while increasing others that they consider to be more sustainable, and start making new distinctions about whom to buy from. For example, the purchase of a cup of coffee used to be a simple 50-cent expenditure and there were only a few brands to choose from—Folgers, Maxwell House, and Sanka. Today, coffee drinkers are concerned about "fair-trade," "rain-forest friendly," "organic," "shade tree grown," and shipped by clean-fuel-burning trucks. An even better example is the increase in locally grown (note the birth of the term *locavore*), fair-trade, and organic produce that is sweeping the nation.

Consumers want to know where a product comes from, how it's packaged, how it's shipped, who the distributors and suppliers are, and what their processes are. Smart Green companies respond to this informed consumer demand by adapting their internal and external processes to align with sustainability principles. They in turn demand similar changes from their direct relationships or change to new ones that match their new level of greenth (in this case a Leaf). Their product life cycle becomes realigned with a new pathway from the product's creation to its disposal to have less negative impact on the environment; and the company realizes newfound revenues and profits from a growing market and a product differentiator. To be clear, a company that adapts its product and processes to meet new consumer demand, as well as aligning itself with companies at a similar level of greenth, has essentially improved upon the old products and processes. In most cases, the changes that occur are considered merely "less bad" rather than actually "good" for the environment. No doubt over time as components of the web of relationships in each sector achieve a higher level of greenth, adaptations will become truly sustainable.

The complexity of the web of relationships within each sector prohibits an overnight change, but, as in nature, adaptation through incremental change over time is a powerful tool that finally tips the scale toward the change that makes the most sense ecologically, socially, and financially.

SUSTAINABLE STRATEGY 2: PLASTICITY

Like the concept of adaptation in nature, plasticity is a scientific concept (in this case from brain research) that has significant implications as a tool for developing your sustainability strategy. Recent studies in brain research have discovered fascinating properties of the brain, such as its ability to grow new neuron pathways where they didn't exist before to accommodate opportunities for growth and learning as in developing infants; for recovering from traumatic events such as an automobile accident or a stroke where portions of the brain have been damaged; and for maintaining lucidity and better memory as people age.

For infants and toddlers, the neurons are being created at an exponential rate; for this brief period in the human life cycle, learning new things is as natural as breathing. Brain plasticity is at its highest point early in life when we can least remember it. Our ability to learn to adapt to changes is developed during the first five years of life and is very difficult to alter once this period has passed. That is why it's easier for young children to learn to speak foreign languages and play musical instruments and more difficult for adults.

For someone who has had a brain trauma where many regions of the brain for specific functions such as speech and cognition were damaged, the road back to health is long and arduous. Researchers have found that if the brain is stimulated in specific ways, many of the functions that were lost return, even though a fraction of the brain remains! When the brain is stimulated to respond, new neurons are being created to form new pathways in the remaining sections of the brain. As people age, researchers recommend keeping the mind and body as active as possible to continue the pattern of neuron growth, maintaining and increasing memory capacity and, most important, the ability to think, dream, and innovate.

Plasticity in brain research is mirrored in developing your company's sustainability strategy. Whereas adaptation is changing the development process and components, products, and business relationships with other companies to align more with customer demand from one level of greenth to another, plasticity is changing the company and product to something altogether different whose process and components may not even exist yet (see Figure 4.6). There will likely be a changing pattern of relationships, product life cycle, and profitability for the new company.

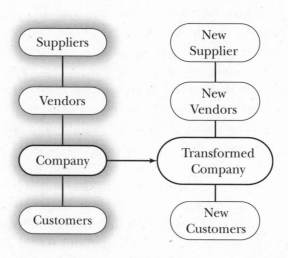

Figure 4.6   Plasticity

A Smart Green company that utilizes the principle of plasticity as a tool for its sustainability strategic plan will soon realize it is marching to a different drummer. The basic assumptions of what a product is, how it is made, how it is shipped, how it is sold, how it is used, and how it is disposed of all have to be redefined in the context of no harm to the environment, enhancing the quality of life of individuals, and new concepts of the meaning of wealth. Like the grown-up trying to learn a new language or the brain trauma patient trying to regain her ability to speak, existing companies will have a harder time implementing a plasticity approach, but that's not to say it's impossible. A new economic model, business case, suppliers, distributors, vendors, and even professional service providers that comprehend and support the new model will help in the transformation. The process of plasticity occurs naturally in nature as long as there is stimulus to the brain for the neurons to form. There has to be an incentive, a motive, and repetition of action for the new pathways to be created.

Entrepreneurs starting new companies are like the child from birth through age five: They have the ability to learn and apply new concepts and modes of thinking at an alarming rate with fewer barriers to change than existing companies face. Today the products don't exist to fuel our cars without harm to the environment, but because of the principle of plasticity, we will be able to develop them. "Necessity is the mother of invention" is now "Opportunity is the mother of innovation."

To be clear, plasticity is not a process of changing out old products for new ones, like trading in your SUV for a Prius; it's redefining the car itself, our relationship with the automobile and the symbol of freedom and mobility it represents. Multiplied by six billion people, even the most fuel-efficient car is not sustainable. Plasticity is also not a call for a return to nature, abandoning all of our stuff for a simpler, wealthless existence. Rather, it's an opportunity to reinvent ourselves and our stuff in new ways that enrich our lives and the lives of others, and to make our world a better place for our descendants to realize their dreams as well as for the plants and creatures with which we share the planet.

THE SEVEN TIERS OF SMART GREEN GROWTH

The Smart Green Strategic Planning Framework includes seven tiers of growth that any number of categories of targeted groups, products, or processes will pass through, beginning with the awareness tier and ending with the innovation tier. Understanding the implication of each tier is critical for every aspect of your enterprise, including management, finance, training, leadership development, facilities management, and marketing and sales. Each tier is progressive, describes a particular mind-set required, and has metrics and properties to collect and report on; and beyond the planning process, the framework can be developed into a scorecard for each of the categories chosen for your strategic plan. Before starting this process of growth, you have to first be interested. This is the stage for even starting on these seven tiers because there has been no tipping point to encourage a desire to change.

An example is the owner of a medium-sized landscaping and lawn care company. Landscaping companies have many hurdles to overcome to become more sustainable, but the potential to make significant changes to the environment is great. Very labor intensive, high water requirements, dependent upon heavy equipment and trucks, favoring use of herbicides, pesticides, and fertilizers, a single company with a 100 clients can produce a massive negative footprint to higher CO_2 levels and cumulative negative on consumer property. With so much opportunity for change, most landscaping and lawn care companies have not made significant changes to their products and services. The owner has not heard many requests for more sustainable property management except for lower water level requirements due to recent droughts. As soon as the rains came, though, those customers pulled their request. The margins are very tight and competition fierce for basic lawn care so any changes to the status quo means higher prices to the customer. Also, suppliers and nurseries are not feeling the demand from their buyers yet either so very few new products have been introduced into the market. "It's a customer-driven market," says the owner. "I'll be happy to change our practices and products but I want to stay in business first." A few organic nurseries are beginning to crop up and some natural fertilizers and pesticides are emerging into the market slowly. Landscaping companies with fore-sight will likely see a windfall soon as customer opinion changes. Once the change occurs to seek out a new sustainable strategy, the company is ready to begin the journey. What follows are basic descriptions of the seven tiers of Smart Green growth.

Tier One: Awareness of the Need for Change

Once you have experienced a tipping point from the explosion of information from the Green Rush and determined that sustainabil-ity is a goal that requires a change of mind-set rather than just being an interesting topic to explore, you are in the tier of awareness. Prior to initiating any strategies or having specific knowledge about sus-tainability, there is a growing sense of a change of mind-set that you need to address. Oftentimes we experience hearing bits and pieces of important information that begins to develop a schema or context for the inevitable need for change that is to come. Your attributes in this tier of awareness include openness to new possibilities, deter-mination in the face of adversity for trying new approaches, and a relentless desire to pursue more information and to learn from men-tors. The pitfall of this tier is the fear of change. Many will resist the inclination to pursue any more information because the changes seem insurmountable; you may be afraid of the implications of the changes required; you are so distracted with current activities that you fail to find the necessary time to reflect; or you ultimately decide that your own status and belief of what you think and do are right. So you stop because you recognize that the changes may be severe and the road ahead is rough. Your benefit in this tier is the realiza-tion that your can contribute to the betterment of the environment and to social equity, and continually strive for growth and profit in the expanding global community.

One example of becoming aware of the need for change is Richard Johanson, a recent graduate from the University of North Carolina at Chapel Hill. The university environment provides a rich opportunity to explore new approaches to sustainability and today most institutions of higher learning are vying vigorously for students based on how green they are. The Univerisity of NC at Chapel Hill has emerged as a national leader in many aspects of its sustainability strategic planning from its LEED Platinum building and other LEED certified buildings to the Institute for Sustainable Enterprise through the business school and many initiatives across campus to strive towards sustainable practices. Richard Johanson, a senior graduating from UNC-CH in Political Science and Sustainability, began four and half years ago, and sustainability was never on his radar screen. "I noticed that the campus was making efforts like waterless urinals and removing styrofoam in the cafeterias. When I entered college, I thought sustainability was more of a 'hippie' fad, but now I see it as an important theme of my Carolina education. I thought that I would graduate and go to law school, but I have recently become interested in business and sustainable solutions consulting. Several influences guided me to become more aware of the issues and enhanced my understanding of sustainability principles: Professors began adding sustainability issues to their curricula; the campus attracted great speakers on the subject; and the Chapel Hill community has been very active in sustainable practices, providing internship and educational opportunities. Though sustainability has gradually become more mainstream on campus, there continues to be polarization between those students who care a lot about sustainability and those who are not as concerned. Having read about corporate social responsibility in the business community, I'm hoping to choose a position at a company that matches my sustainability consciousness. I have been lucky enough to find several companies which align with my interests. My advice to the University in retrospect: Because the issue is so important, administrators could do more to educate students early on about the University's sustainability initiatives and how students can get involved. The economic downturn has certainly made the job search process more difficult. It is a tough time to be trying to enter the workforce."

Tier Two: Recognition of Implications

In this tier, you have become aware of key facts and implications about sustainability that may or may not affect the business. Although the specific issues and strategies are unclear, there is a knowledge of everything seeming important and that something certainly needs to change. As the information builds up and the schema it has created begins to show a pattern, finally a catalyst brings it into perspective. This catalyst could be a quote, a report, a global event, a mentor's comment, a personal experience—something that confirms that not only is there a trend, but you need to either adapt or lead your company into the next phase. The four attributes in this tier are excitement, action orientation, a new level of caring based on new-found knowledge, and commitment to seeing the process through to the end. The pitfall of this tier is acting without thinking. Many of you may become fixated on a single solution and not take into account all of the possible implications of a single action. In your enthusiasm, you will champion the cause without bringing everyone along with you, and will misinterpret lack of participation as lack of interest from your peers or employees. Your benefits in this tier are the passion, energy, and focus to accomplish a goal that encompasses a broader range of outcomes, as well as the willingness to take risks that may have been out of the question before.

Ann Westergaard has been a successful Shaklee Distributor for 36 years. The Shaklee Corporation is a global company that manufactures and distributes natural nutritional supplements, beauty products, and cleaning supplies. The company began over 50 years ago by Dr. Forrest C. Shaklee and was the first to introduce the concept of network marketing, as well as being the first Carbon Neutral company in the world, long before it was considered popular. Ann joined Shaklee at first to improve her health and soon fell in love with its environmental principles, having been raised by a conservationist and a professor who were concerned about pollutants in the rivers. As the years progress, Ann's passion has been to teach people how to develop better health and non-toxic homes: one house at a time. The most striking aspect of Shaklee Ann mentions is "They walk their talk."

Network Marketing is becoming one of the fastest growing business models in the country. Members are able to purchase products at retail or at a discount if they "share" the business with others to become members as well. As they increase members in their "downline," a percentage of the sales flows back up the sponsoring member. Products are drop shipped and some forward-thinking companies such as Shaklee Corp. provide carbon offsets for shipments in the form of planting trees. At the recent conference in New Orleans, Shaklee replaced CO_2's to balance the participants' travel impact. Shaklee's CEO, Roger Barnett, has a goal of eliminating malnutrition worldwide. Shaklee makes a difference in the world by empowering individuals and families to not only lead healthy lives but also make a living through their social marketing plan. Individuals do not have to have a lot of money to make a change in the world. "I enjoy being part of something bigger than I am. I'm in my 70s and earn $100K at home and am surrounded by friends. How many people can say that? My greatest challenge is finding people who are open and willing to learn and try new things. I look forward to meeting the next person who will share this concept with their friends. I believe we are making a difference!"

Tier Three: Analysis of Current State

In this tier, you begin the process of analyzing your current state of awareness—your level of greenth as well as each of the social, economic, and environmental issues facing your community. You will explore consumer demands and stakeholder expectations and do an assessment of each element of the total company footprint. Whereas in the previous tier you were ready to take a leap before looking, in this tier you are taking a good look for the purpose of bringing everyone critical to the enterprise along for sufficient buy-in and support to get started with an initiative. Your attributes in this tier are to be self-disciplined, detached, patient, analytical, and market-driven. The pitfall of this tier is becoming so data-driven that you see everything as a number. Many will fall into the trap of providing substantiated proof and statistics of the current state of the company, the community, the region, and what the customers may be looking for, but the intuition to understand human dynamics and the way various issues are connected organically may be lost. Again, a new solution may be arrived at prematurely without the hands-on experience of meeting with people, piloting an initiative before rolling it out, and relying too much on the numbers. The benefit of this tier is self-reflection as individuals take the time to analyze themselves and your organization from a third-person perspective.

"Switching to organic farming is not going to make me rich," says an Orange County, NC farmer who began converting her 2.4 acre farm four years ago to produce only organic vegetables, free range eggs and hormone free chickens. To be certified organic, the land must be free of contaminates for several years and tested before any products can be labeled as such. The demand for local, organic vegetables, eggs, chickens, hogs, beef, cheese, and milk is increasing in North Carolina but the prices and scaleability of small farms is conducive for only subsistence living. "It's a labor of love for us. We believe we are providing a service and following our convictions." Area co-ops, restaurants, and traditional grocery stores are including more local produce than ever before. As the demand increases, perhaps there will be sufficient investment available to increase the size of the farms and take advantage of the benefits of organic farming on a larger scale.

As another example, the building industry has likely seen the greatest changes in recent years towards the introduction of a variety of sustainability-related products from forest-friendly timber, to recycled insulation, passive solar panels, and Energy Star appliances. A "green home" can mean a hundred different things because there are currently no standards. In the facilities management field, LEED certifications are driving many of the high rise and big box facilities nationwide. Every supplier to the building industry is under pressure to redesign themselves in the image of sustainability, with little or no guidance except reduction of carbon emissions and recycling. Architects and engineers are enjoying a new cottage industry from large corporations desiring to create the image of how green they are by building all new structures from sustainable principles. A great side benefit to green buildings in the commercial sector is the correlation to improved employee performance, retention, and attraction to the company. Organizations that invest in sustainable buildings gain a bigger bang for their buck than just saved energy costs. One facilities manager is wary of the enthusiasm: "The cost of LEED certification is high and we have a tight budget as it is. I can't tell if we are getting a plaque on the wall and a press release on the website with a lot of capital tied up in getting certified. There are many other high-risk projects we need to be investing in at this time as well." Like the landscaping sector, the building industry has an enormous footprint with the amount of raw material used for a single facility or home that affects many diverse companies. Changes towards sustainable practice in this sector reverberates through many others.

Tier Four: Applying a Systems View Approach

In this tier, a great leap of trust from you is required. You may have the passion, knowledge, analytical information, and great ideas for a strategy and marketing plan for your company's direction, but unless your efforts are placed within the context of a greater system—the larger footprint being left by your suppliers, vendors, customers, and partners—you will not have the desired impact on the triple bottom line, and your customers will figure that out sooner or later. This is a key point of departure in deciding to take the path of adaptation or that of plasticity—that is, either to change the existing products to be greener or to re-create the product from scratch. A new strategic plan must be developed that incorporates the three systems views: the production cycle, the relationships within the footprint, and the business case. Your attributes in this tier are to be systems-oriented, have a long-term view, and be focused on sustainability impacts, especially the bottom line. The pitfall for you in this tier is failing to realize your true potential. You may not take the risk of changing all of your processes and products to meet your dream of becoming fully sustainable, because deep down you are afraid of the time it will take or the increased chance of failure. Every step of the way requires more commitment and creativity to innovate than anything you've done before. You just have to trust your feelings, knowledge, the system and how it works, and your own ability to call upon creativity when it is needed. The benefit to you in this tier is to finally see the long view of your beliefs and awareness of what is possible with your company and the team you've hired to accomplish your goals with whichever path (adaptation or plasticity) you choose.

Tier Five: Planning and Implementing a Strategy

Once the choice is made about which path to follow, in this tier you take the first step in developing a comprehensive strategic plan in the form of a pilot to test the waters of their product ideas. In the business context, a new web forms in the production, relationship, and business case cycles, each of which is being tested and analyzed for efficiency and effectiveness. The outcomes are potentially more evident and costs are increasingly justifiable as the payback period becomes manageable. Once data comes back from the pilot, you can analyze the results for potential rollout. Your attributes in this tier are leadership, courage, detail orientation, and good communication. The pitfall of this tier is failure to manage the complexity. You may become hyper-focused on the objectives and steps of the project and not realize how many people and issues need to be managed and issues resolved that have not been encountered before. There will likely be more stakeholders, more alliances to be maintained, greater diversity of staff, more implications for each decision that have to be unpacked, more financial relationships that have to be worked out with an increasing number of inexperienced negotiators, and more knowledge of sustainability impacts to report on. The benefit to you in this tier is the experience of leading others and managing complexity while maintaining a higher vision long enough to see results—for better or for worse.

Tier Six: Analysis of and Reflection on Outcomes and Impacts

In this tier the data begins to roll in and the information is new, scary, and exhilarating. Your project may have failed. Perhaps the results are so different from what you have experienced that it's difficult to maintain a straight course. This is where extra trust in the vision of wise strategic planning and goal setting and adjustments must be maintained as the new pathways and relationships begin to form and take shape. The attributes for you in this tier include courage, perseverance, trust, and belief. The pitfall for this tier is that the truth hurts. Many of your colleagues may balk at the changes because it's difficult to keep up, or perhaps the financial impact is either taking too long or is not good enough. Many members of your team, investors, and partners might decide to leave because they can't take the heat of failure or uncertainty. Some may view the incoming analytics reports and realize how granular the results are, revealing that performance is below the accepted benchmark. Great care is needed in keeping your core group and stakeholders up to speed and motivated during this period of reflection and growth. The benefit for you in this tier is a tougher skin and fearlessness—to be able to look at the true outcomes of business value and decisively take the next course of action.

Tier Seven: Innovation, Creativity, Growth, and Meaning

In this tier, you remember why you became an entrepreneur in the first place. We have very few opportunities in our lives to create something from nothing or chart a course into undiscovered territory with a merry band of companions. Business is one of the last venues to experience the exhilaration of shared vision, companionship, discovery, and innovation. As the systems become more intertwined and new business relationships continue to expand, suddenly wealth is growing, too. Meanwhile, you are possibly making a difference in the world—through meaningful employment of like-minded people with great wages; a wildly creative environment for new ways of working, selling, and creating products and services; significantly less waste added to the environment; possible contribution to the power grid; and a visible connection to the web of life itself.

CATEGORIES FOR THE STRATEGIC PLANNING FRAMEWORK

Now that you have explored the attributes, pitfalls, and benefits of the seven tiers of Smart Green growth, the next step in developing your Smart Green strategic plan is to identify those categories for which you will chart progress and level of greenth if they apply to stakeholders and business relationships. The purpose of these categories is to provide a means to identify where each of the category items may land within the tier structure in order to be able to analyze the item for strategic planning. There are four basic categories: stakeholders, business relationships, product life cycle, and sustainability outcomes.

First, stakeholders are all those individuals and groups that have the power to support or contend with you on every decision.

They require management, education, and decisive leadership if you are embarking on significant change through the tiers. Stakeholders could include investors, the board of directors, the CEO, your management team, your line managers, and employees.

Second, your business relationships include all of those individuals and organizations on which you depend in order to stay in business. These same business relationships have the power to not buy from you, not sell to you, or support you to enormous success. They require constant management, marketing, education, and clarity of vision as you progress through the tiers. Business relationships include customers, vendors, partners, suppliers, distributors, professional service providers, the community at large, and the public sector for compliance and for partnerships.

Third, the product life cycle is the critical path your product takes from extraction to its disposal. It must be analyzed and managed carefully as an image of your company's commitment to sustainability. As more customers demand more transparency regarding product life cycle, you have to be willing to share accurate, meaningful information about the efforts you are progressively making to have an impact on the entire life cycle eventually. The product life cycle could include extraction, transport, refinement, manufacturing, distribution, retail, consumption, and disposal or reuse.

Fourth, as with product life cycle, customers need more transparency on the outcomes of environment impact, social equity, and profits. The list of metrics defining the outcomes for sustainability is enormous and requires careful consideration for reporting on only those issues that will serve the purpose of the goals and success of your company. Many of the items on the list will be part of certification programs that have been predetermined, and you may want to customize the list to enhance those impacts you are having greatest effect on or that customers are demanding. For example, environmental impacts may take the form of effects on air, water, land, energy, waste, flora and fauna, and human health; potential metrics include changes in CO_2 levels, water use and groundwater levels, land use and value, conservation of land use, energy efficiency, percentage of alternative energy sources, reduce/recycle/reuse practices and waste alternatives, preservation of habitat, protection of birds and amphibians, and improvements in community health as indicated by weight and illnesses such as cancer, diabetes, and heart disease. Social impacts could include support of community organizations, employment with living wage, community development initiatives, arts and education, economic development, and participation in regional initiatives. Profitability impacts could include profit, growth, return on investment (ROI) to investors, bonuses to employees, taxes paid to the state and federal government, and reinvestment into sustainable innovations.

The relationship between these categories and the seven tiers of Smart Green growth can be used as the core working document for your sustainability strategic plan. You can assign a time line, budget, and task manager to the list in your own format. I have found that importing the tiers and the categories into any project management system provides the necessary framework. The next chapter takes the strategic plan and outlines the processes by which Smart Green companies apply measurement approaches such as analytics to demonstrate greater transparency and accurate reporting of sustainability outcomes.

YOUR STRATEGIC ROAD MAP

You now have all the tools for developing your Smart Green strategic plan. The next step is to use a road map for getting to your destination, taking all that you have learned about the Green Rush, the triple bottom line, your level of greenth, the seven tiers of Smart Green change, your understanding of your placement within the economic biosphere, and whether you will use adaptation or plasticity as your response to new market opportunities. This road map begins the next step of your development beyond outdated and out-of-sync models of planning and implementation, because many of the rules have changed and the outcomes have been expanded beyond financial metrics alone as the measure of success.

If you remember from Chapter 2 the five stages of change model that introduced the idea that you may be in many different stages of change at once, depending on what issue you are speaking about, and that it's common to recycle through one stage or another as you experience failure or disillusionment. By this time you are in the maintenance stage of change and less likely to be recycling through the stage of wondering whether going green is a fad or a megatrend, or whether you care about the environment and your active participation to community empowerment, or whether your company needs to take action on sustainability.

Most strategic planning models traditionally used in corporate settings and for long-range planning of organizations and institutions fail to include many of the necessary dimensions required in the new Age of Sustainability. Some models just add social equity and environmental stewardship as new line items to report on without consideration of much deeper issues and wider implications that are required in sustainability planning. The next-generation model for strategic planning requires more categories and stages to accommodate the number of issues and concerns that must be addressed for you to be successful.

5

Measuring Sustainability Outcomes

Courage is not the absence of fear, but the capacity for action despite our fears.

—*John McCain*

What you risk reveals what you value.

—*Jeanette Winterson*

THE MOON SHOT

Having developed a sustainability strategic plan and identified target areas in which to implement sustainability projects throughout your enterprise, it is imperative to tie all of your initiatives into a sustainability measurement plan. Smart Green companies don't rely on gut feelings or "spray and pray" methods of deployment with customer satisfaction sheets as the only means for determining the business value of their investment; too much is at stake. General Motors announced in the summer of 2008 that it was "going for a moon shot" by delivering a viable electric vehicle (in production and ready for sale) by the end of 2010, a monumental feat since it takes four to five years to introduce a new *normal* vehicle. The automaker's metrics will be delivery on time, quality product, and sales. Employees interviewed feel that through their success they can change the world.

The Green Rush has had a major impact on many companies as they revisit their business plans for aggressive sustainability strategies. This is a good sign as long as they move beyond the image of sustainability to the results of sustainability, a reservation voiced by Mikko Valtonen of Proventia Solutions: "There are lots of pictures of butterflies, lakes, and mountains, because often these [sustainability] reports are prepared by environmentally focused employees in the public-relations department," who are more interested in promoting a pro-green image.[1]

Many of the concepts discussed here of developing a strategic plan, exploring the differences between savings on investment (SOI) and return on investment (ROI), and connecting the strategic planning process to the development of a business case are derived from my own experiences in starting businesses. Some of the executives I interviewed indicated a desire to measure their companies' success in new ways, but always keeping an eye on the bottom line.

For example, "Success with sustainability depends on whether it is profitable and if you feel good about what you are doing," says Bob Hartford of Silverwood Bingham Ridge, a solar home developer. While others I spoke with simply don't have a plan to measure. Paul Toma of Common Ground just recently opened his store, and he's not yet clear on how he plans on measuring sustainability. Many of the other groups measure their success not by financial methods but based on nonfinancial results such as the increase in the number of members of a sustainable building council or an energy consortium. One creative response to how you measure sustainability is: "Our greatest responsibility is to be good ancestors."

MEASURING BUSINESS VALUE

The bottom line. Nothing in business communicates more about a company's success than what is reported at the end of the day, at the end of the month, at the end of the quarter, at year's end, and over three years, depending upon what stakeholder perspective you are coming from. But the bottom line is no longer the best indicator of success. Periodic gains in growth and profit are now being cast in the light of social inequities and environmental disasters, so we have to recalibrate our thinking to understand that we as a global community are all in this together and must be working together for mutual success and sustainability. We have to redefine what business value is: return on investment, both financial and nonfinancial, on strategic aspects of the triple bottom line that are relevant for the sustainable growth of an organization.

Over the past 10 years I have measured the business impact of a variety of departments using statistical analysis tools. Because the tools reveal true financial value in isolation from other activities, I have noticed that the method is met with consistent resistance from managers whose projects don't perform as well as expected even though there may be a lot of enthusiasm for those projects. But recently I've noticed a change. More and more, there is great interest from managers from every department to measure ROI, because upper management is demanding it. Upper management wants to rely more on measurable financial outcomes and less on anecdotal data or dashboards that display the current state but do not isolate the impact. Also, more data is being collected than ever before and there are more opportunities for calculating business impact, isolating a project's business value, and optimizing strategies for greater return.

I have found that the main use of collecting data for business intelligence is to display the data in the form of dashboards to show current state rather than true analysis of what is producing results and what is causing the company to bleed. The main lesson learned from the past 10 years of measuring business impact is that most businesses don't really measure return on investment, and should. Furthermore, when companies do measure ROI and don't like what they see, they stop measuring it. Return on investment is most effectively measured by an analytics process (explained later in this chapter) rather than through subjective interviews, and planning for measurement is always the last item on the budget and first item to be cut. These lessons come from experience of having measured business impact for dozens of organizations, both public and private, in a variety of departments, including training, human resources (HR), information technology (IT), facilities management, procurement, marketing and sales, and support call centers.

Today, the stakes are higher than ever before to demonstrate this new vision of business value. Even with the most open and willing employees, a sustainability strategic plan cannot survive the scrutiny of stakeholders, the impatience of even the most patient socially responsible investors, and, hardest of all, the informed but fickle customer without a transparent, analytics-based measurement plan that demonstrates return on investment from actual data. Dashboards and interviews aside, Smart Green companies measure business impact, monitor strategic decisions, adjust their strategies accordingly, and maximize their return on all outcomes of the triple bottom line.

Times are tough everywhere. Every company is increasingly finding it difficult to compete in the global economy. This isn't a negative environment for conducting business; rather, it's a level playing field and an opportunity for creativity, innovation, visionaries, and smart planning to arise and thrive. Smart Green companies are smart because they rely on updated, meaningful information to base their decisions on and they are vigilant in increasing or at least maintaining market share while transparently decreasing their negative impact on the environment or creating a new product model altogether with zero impact.

In recent years, many organizations have begun to rely on using analytics—quantitative and statistical analysis of data—and have successfully applied the results to strategic decisions. According to Mikko Valtonen in *CFO* magazine, "Companies are realizing that they must now report on a wide range of nonfinancial indicators, but those same indicators have genuine financial impact, so they want to integrate this sustainability data into their daily operations." Analytics for measurement of business outcomes is becoming a business imperative: "Many previous bases for competition—such as geographical advantage or protective regulation—have been eroded by globalization. Proprietary technologies are rapidly copied, and breakthrough innovations in products or services are increasingly difficult to achieve. That leaves three things as the basis for competition: efficient and effective execution, smart decision making, and the ability to wring every last drop of value from business processes—all of which can be gained through sophisticated use of analytics."[2]

Though this trend of measuring business impact with an analytics approach is rising, most organizations still collect mountains of data and fail to use adequate tools to measure ROI. They also must broaden the measurement of impact for outcomes that indicate positive changes in the social and environmental aspects that can be also be associated with profitability. Thriving, sustainable companies are strategic, practical, and methodical in justifying costs of every investment, including social equity and environmental stewardship.

In facilities management, for example, there are increasing amounts of data being collected and more efforts being made to understand the current state of the operation through visible dashboards. In addition, more managers want to further assess the business impact of facilities operations but may not know how to do so or may lack the necessary management support to use sophisticated analytics tools to measure return on investment. Ask facilities managers about what metrics are currently being used to indicate business value, and they may tell you that their list includes customer satisfaction sheets, time-on-task reports, monitoring of trouble tickets, cost savings through smart procurement, and in some cases, online dashboards indicating the current state of organizational operations.

Many managers are clear that they need to market themselves more effectively, as the perception from upper management is that their departments are ripe for budget cuts. In several interviews conducted with facilities managers, they explain they have a "lack of power in the organization to influence change." Some feel there is "too much emphasis on cost containment initiatives such as Six Sigma and process improvement and not enough on investments to improve productivity." Others see a diminishing return as a result: "Even though my costs of services have gone down from year to year, I have also had a diminishing budget consistently from year to year. I have cut further to balance out shortfalls of cash from other departments."

For all business leaders across all sectors, the benefit of discerning and applying the difference between cost savings and return on investment will also empower them to implement a sustainability strategic plan more effectively.

SAVINGS ON INVESTMENT AND RETURN ON INVESTMENT

Before an analytics process can be implemented and the right metrics identified, let's compare apples with apples. One great misconception about measuring business impact that affects selecting metrics is that cost savings on the budget is considered a return on investment (ROI) when in actuality a savings on investment (SOI) is being realized.

The typical SOI approach defines value to the organization in two basic ways: cuts to the budget and improvement of organizational processes. The highest forms of SOI activities include mass economies of scale, hyperefficiency, and business processes that reduce waste and time, such as Six Sigma initiatives. Though a necessary step for maximizing resources available, SOI analysis alone is a process of diminishing returns that seeks to solve short-term goals, may misinterpret business drivers of clients, and potentially fails to inspire break-through value for the organization.

The ROI of a project or groups of projects assumes a measurable financial return that is measured by an analytics process. Measuring business impact requires statistical analysis to isolate the benefit from other possible inputs to the benefit. In contrast to SOI, ROI relies on greater connectivity and communication between interacting departments—a systems view demonstrating alignment with the strategic goals of the organization.

The greatest benefit of an ROI analysis is that through careful identification of intervention and control groups, departments can tease out additional information to optimize their strategies and deploy the projects across the enterprise for even greater return. Long considered too expensive, too complicated, or downright impossible, measuring business benefit not only is possible, but it is fast becoming a business imperative.

INCREASING BUSINESS VALUE AWARENESS

Business value services take two main forms, one educational and one analytical. The whole effort to measure the business value of a particular activity or initiative requires a lot of paradigm shifting within each level of management, as almost nobody is used to thinking about their job in this way.

The first stage of involvement emphasizes the educational end of the spectrum to ensure that a core team has a basic level of business value awareness so that each key milestone of a project is being designed and implemented with eventual measurability in mind.

Business value awareness is the understanding of the impact of an activity far beyond that surface level—on the teams, departments, divisions, and, ultimately, organizations that we are part of. Every organization or company has a small number of goals it is committed to: creating a particular set of products or experiences, with a particular level of quality, and, perhaps, generating a particular level of profit. All of the tasks carried on by every individual in the organization are the fine details of endeavor that add up to those few strategic goals. Business value awareness is the understanding of the purpose of all of these individual tasks as ingredients in delivering these strategic goals.

Doing a good job of setting ROI metrics doesn't begin with data collection—there are design principles through the whole project that will benefit the value measures collected later. This process of education would be a big part of the alignment of stakeholders, as well; few people are accustomed to the open sharing of goals and data that are required across departments/partnering companies to make ROI-level metrics meaningful.

THE ANALYTICS APPROACH

The key to a successful evaluation of a project is to distinguish between an evaluation based on assumptions and one based on statistical analysis. While interviews and customer satisfaction sheets are useful as reflections of attitudes of constituents or clients, these outcomes do not indicate the impact of the project on the organization as a whole. Neither do assessments of knowledge change (testing) and behavior change (skill development). An analytics approach answers these five critical questions:

1. What was the return on investment?

2. What difference did it make to the agency's strategic goals?

3. What worked best and for whom?

4. What is the best deployment strategy for the project being measured?

5. What could the potential benefit be for future years and for other regions?

At times, these questions can challenge even the status quo of various departments during a change that requires an honest look at value. Engineers from a pharmaceutical company were concerned

Table 5.1 Measurement Differences between Smart Green and Greenwashing Companies

Smart Green Measurement	Greenwashing Measurement
Analytics-Based Measurement: Statistics	Assumptions-Based Measurement: Opinions
Financial Outcomes	Subjective Outcomes
Strategic: Long-Term	Tactical: Short-Term
Return on Investment (ROI)	Savings on Investment (SOI)
Continuous Growth, Best Practices	Maintain Status Quo, Current Practices

about budget cuts following the merger with another company. In trying to demonstrate their value as internal experts with institutional knowledge that made a difference in designing state-of-the-art research facilities, they failed to realize the need to demonstrate their value where routine building maintenance (functions easily outsourced) was available. Some of the engineers were aware of the dilemma—that they needed to reduce their numbers and change their roles, a difficult position when jobs are on the line.

As Table 5.1 indicates, when two assessment styles—assumptions-based and analytics-based—are compared, the latter approach provides a view that is normally seen by upper management—a necessary shift of mind-set for managers to more effectively demonstrate their value.

Managers need a third-person perspective, as business value analysts, with the right tools and approaches to demonstrate their value, becoming a strategic partner in long-term decision making and a facilitator of growth for the organization.

Since measuring with analytics is dependent upon this change in mind-set, choosing the right metrics becomes increasingly important. In one recent example, a government agency requested three bids from organizations providing ergonomically designed workstations. The criteria included best price, most mobility, and approval by the employees as measured over six weeks by the same group of employees using the workstations two weeks at a time. Though the agency may get the best price of a mobile system that employees enjoy, from an analytics perspective these criteria fail to address the true benefit of the purchase: impact on productivity. In this scenario, besides the cost savings from choosing the cheapest workstations, the metrics and the design to measure them are subjective. In an analytics approach, each workstation would be deployed to three employee groups with generally the same function. Instead of collecting employee satisfaction sheets, productivity levels would be measured and compared— between the groups and from the previous month's performance.

CHOOSING THE RIGHT METRICS

Why is an analytics process—using statistics to determine value— necessary for managers? No other objective tools are available to adequately isolate the business impact of facilities management activities. The concepts of intervention groups and control groups are integral to ensuring adequate comparisons of changes in performance and behavior of building occupants and systems. The data required for an analytics process is already being gathered and stored, but modeling and analyzing the data require planning, foresight, and the right questions.

Managers who consider measuring the ROI of their projects or other aspects of their budgets begin the process by entering a process of changing some of their mind-set about an analytics approach. First, they need to become oriented to organizational and departmental strategies and match projects to the business goals that will be expected to impact at both levels. A process similar to the Balanced Scorecard could help with this.

Next, managers identify metrics for these expected business value impacts and establish potential intervention and control groups that best demonstrate the isolated impact of the project intervention (e.g., different floors or buildings with the same type of employee, pre- and post-intervention data, etc.). These metrics will likely be related to the productivity of building occupants—metrics not usually accessed by managers. New relationships need to be formed to accommodate access to these metrics. Finally, a statistical analysis tool is used, with consultants if necessary, to set up the analysis model, collect the data, and analyze the results.

Data for this type of analysis are of three types: participants (who is receiving the benefits of the project), performance metrics (what productivity results are being collected), and intervention (project). Each of these data types is required to effectively measure the business impact of facilities management initiatives.

The metrics collected for this type of study would need to be looked at in terms of dollars in order to establish an ROI. Not all metrics can be converted to this form, such as changes in behavior or perception of a project, but the analysis of the data can still be statistical. In the case example later in the chapter, the result of this type of study helps to establish a more reliable strategic decision in the purchase of new lighting. If the best price is the only consideration, all the benefits of increased sales and less sick leave might be lost—which could amount to millions of dollars. Moreover, the cost of this type of analysis is paid back many times over by taking the information and applying it to multiple facilities of the same type—known as optimization.

Many hidden benefits and potential losses can be discovered by using this type of methodology. The delivery of outcomes for management is in the form of a business case, and the results from the study are more substantiated and believable than the results of a company-wide survey asking employee opinions. The benefit of the manager choosing the right metrics and the right measurement approach is the newfound control of business drivers for the department, strategic partnerships with its internal clients, and a growth facilitator for the organization as a whole.

THE SMART GREEN BUSINESS CASE

So, what is a business case and why is it so important? A business case is a reporting tool utilized mostly by internal managers that outlines the actions, methods, measurement model, outcomes, and recommendations of a strategy implemented within an organization. The report is customarily used to justify the expenditure of a line item in a budget or new initiative to the team and to the stakeholders. For sustainability strategic planning, new dimensions to the outcomes of the business case are included to accommodate the triple bottom line of social, environmental, and financial impacts based on accepted metrics and data sources.

The following case example describes the sustainability strategic planning process for a simple relamping project. In preparation for fulfilling requirements of LEED certification for their facilities, many companies are identifying immediate cost savings through energy reduction, and the low-hanging fruit sometimes includes replacing lighting. In this example, the company is a brokerage firm based in New York City that has dozens of floors throughout several buildings. A change in lighting could provide the company with hundreds of thousands of dollars in cost savings and provide points for its LEED certification. The company has decided to develop a pilot program first in one building before rolling it out to the other buildings.

Case Example: Acme Financial Company

COMPANY: ACME FINANCIAL CO., NEW YORK, NY

Title: Daylight Bulb Replacement Project

EXECUTIVE SUMMARY

Acme Financial Co. facilities management department is fulfilling the corporate goal of reducing the company's energy costs and demonstrating its sustainability initiatives to investors by adopting the LEED Bronze certification program. The facilities management team proposes to initiate first steps toward certification with a relamping project in one building with two different lightbulbs to ensure energy savings and to test the outcome on the productivity of brokers before final rollout. Cost of installation and bulbs will depend on the outcomes of the pilot program.

INTRODUCTION AND OVERVIEW

For over 30 years, Acme Financial Co. has been providing high-yield financial and brokerage services to clients worldwide. Most of Acme's buildings are located in the greater New York City area and all are over 20 years old. The facilities management department has decided to certify all of the company's buildings at LEED Bronze within three years. In consultation with managers from the various departments, employees have requested many changes to the work environment, especially the lighting, which uses both fluorescent tubes and incandescent bulbs. Some employees complain of headaches, dizziness, sleepiness, and distraction from the fluorescent tubes buzzing. Others have mentioned headaches from some lights being too bright. Since the complaints have been increasing in recent years, the facilities management team is attempting to determine the real causes, investigating alternatives that may solve the problems, and exploring cost-effective options to recommend for budget approval while fulfilling the LEED certification process within an aggressive time line. The facilities management team decided todevelop a strategy of deployment and a model for study and to analyze the results.

ASSUMPTIONS AND METHODS

This study will investigate the cost-benefit ratio and the return on investment of switching from fluorescent tubes to daylight or natural bulbs. Four floors of employees at Acme will be studied, floors 10 and 11 as the intervention group (daylight fluorescent bulbs installed) and floors 14 and 15 as the control group (regular fluorescent bulbs installed). Metrics will be collected for all floors simultaneously over three months as well as similar metrics from the year before during the same period. Measurement of value impact requires metrics from several variables to be calculated: the participants, the metrics, and

(continued)

(*continued*)

the intervention. For the design of the value analytics to succeed, the employees on all floors must be of a similar number,
type, and function to ensure an "all things being equal" study.
Computing the value of the lighting program must ensure certainty that the group of employees receiving the daylight bulbs
does not differ in any important respect from those under the
regular fluorescent lighting. Metrics will be collected as follows
based the three variables mentioned:

Variable 1—Participants

Employee ID numbers for sales and support staff for Acme
Financial Co. on floors 11–12 and 14–15 are recorded.
Employees included in the study must have been working for the
company for at least one year and must remain on the same floor
during the duration of the study. Titles, tenure at the company,
salaries, and previous year salaries are recorded.

Variable 2—Metrics

Employee satisfaction surveys pre- and post-study, number
of sick leave days for each floor by employee, health-care plan
claims, attrition, number leaving the company, monthly sales figures, productivity figures (calls being made, pipeline milestones
being met, etc.), previous year's data during same period, speed
of ramp-up time.

Variable 3—Intervention

Installation of daylight bulbs on floors 10 and 11, installation
of fluorescent bulbs on floors 14 and 15, installation cost of
bulbs by fixture and by floor, annual sustainability costs by fixture and floor, estimated energy costs for each floor, previous
year's energy costs for each floor during same period.

   Once the data is collected, filtered for anomalies, and
screened for accuracy, strategic measures will analyze the data

utilizing statistical algorithms for isolating impact. The following five questions can be answered in this analysis:

1. Is there a significant statistical relationship between regular fluorescent lighting and daylight or natural lighting in the workplace?

2. If so, what effect, if any, does lighting have on the satisfaction, health, attrition, productivity, and financial outcomes of employees at Acme Financial Co.?

3. What are the financial implications of the differences between lighting types based on installation and total cost of ownership, energy costs, sick leave and attrition, and sales revenue?

4. Is there a statistical relationship between employee satisfaction and employee health, attrition, productivity, and financial outcomes?

5. If daylight bulbs prove to be effective in improving financial outcomes, what is the payback period (breakeven point) for daylight bulb installations? What is the internal rate of return? What is the return on investment for a company-wide installation? For the return on investment result, the changes in revenue by each group of floors will be used since it is reflected in financial terms. The ROI is calculated by the formula: ROI = (benefit/cost) − cost × 100. The result is reported as a percentage from which the cost-benefit ratio and payback period are calculated. Confidence in the ROI will be dependent on the degree of certainty that the changing of lighting type had a degree of discrete and isolated impact on changes to the productivity and financial results of the employees. A company-wide model will be developed to indicate gains or losses based on the results of the study.

(continued)

(continued)

RESULTS AND CONCLUSIONS

The results of the study surprised the facilities managers, because there was a more significant difference in the productivity metrics than expected. Overall, the best solution was the installation of fluorescent bulbs that have a daylight tint. Although they cost a little more, with a 95 percent ROI within the first few months of deployment after installation, the additional cost is justified. After splitting the employees into quintiles, another startling result appeared: The newer recruits (less than two years with the firm) had a significant increase in their productivity after the more expensive lamps were placed on their desks. The higher-achieving veterans could probably sell stock out of the back of a parked car in the garage, because their results didn't change no matter what kind of lighting was provided. By investing a few hundred thousand more dollars, the relamping project could increase revenue by 400 percent in a year! In conclusion, the cost savings to the organization over three years is $1.2 million. There was no impact to productivity during the changing of bulbs. ROI on daylight bulbs: 95 percent. Optimization: 400 percent ROI for new employees and lower achievers. Recommendation: daylight desk lamps for new employees and lower achievers.

WHY ANALYTICS MATTERS

As you can see in this example, there is more to measuring outcomes than showing a dashboard of performance of employees as you begin developing a sustainability strategic plan. As a business leader, you need more information about every investment that will maximize the dollars and achieve success in the overall sustainability approach. In this case, the decision to gain LEED certification points, an expensive investment with more than 150,000 bulbs to change, is leveraged by the ability to test the impact of the best deployment of bulbs that maximizes employee performance. This principle has been proven time and again across many similar projects such as improving air quality and moving employees into green facilities that have been built using sustainable materials. Productivity, retention, health, and well-being have all gone up in direct correlation to developing a sustainability strategy.

This connection between companies with a green agenda and productivity with an increased likelihood of profitability has not gone unnoticed by the investment community. Socially responsible investors (SRIs) have been investing more and more dollars into organizations with sustainability agendas, to the tune of $2.71 trillion under management in 2007, over 11 percent of the total amount invested. Nearly one in nine investors today are SRIs who have been enjoying an 18 percent growth rate in their investments from year to year.

Factoring environmental and social variables into the next five-year plan is still new for most companies, but Smart Green companies don't add these onto the end of the report with the customary pictures of happy ducks in a pond and clear mountain streams; rather, they embed their projects as investments that get results. It becomes an imperative within their businesses to be sustainable and to measure the savings on investment and the return on investment, and where appropriate to use an analytics report.

SUSTAINABILITY METRICS

Each of the four categories of the sustainability strategic plan—stakeholders, business relationships, product life cycle, and sustainability outcomes—is dependent on the type of metrics being collected to determine the best result for strategic decisions to be made. Each sector, such as agriculture, communications, transportation, retail, and electronics, has a myriad of possibilities for potential, meaningful metrics. In general, the category of sustainability outcomes has the most potential for being similar than the others because they are increasingly becoming more standardized (see description of the Global Reporting Initiative (GRI) in Chapter 6). Three types of measurement of sustainability outcomes can be deployed initially: benchmarking, cost-benefit analysis, and return on investment.

Benchmarking

There are currently many available indicators for the social, environmental, and economic aspects of the community that can be used as benchmarks for change as your organization begins collecting its own data. For the economic aspect, metrics available are population growth, retail sales, tax base breakdown, per-capita personal income, median family income, unemployment, welfare recipients, housing costs, visitor spending, agricultural (and other sector) spending, and so on.

For the environmental aspect, metrics are air quality (ozone exceedances), water consumption (demand per capita and total demand), green space (residents per acre of protected natural areas), consumption (tons per capita of waste and recyclables), consumption from local electric company, redevelopment versus greenfield development, modal split (transportation modes), multimodal availability, hazardous material inventory and spills, and so on.

For the social aspect, metrics include graduation rate, student/teacher ratios, high school operating expenses, suicide rate, deaths from heart disease, deaths from all cancers, syphilis rate, AIDS rate, percentage of population with health insurance, percentage meeting daily physical activity requirements, home ownership rate, average commute time, percent choosing transit over personal vehicle, child abuse reports, percentage of smokers, population density, violent crime rate, and property crime rate.[3]

Benchmarking from year to year will provide you both the numerator (your metric change) and the denominator (the community metric change) to provide an overall benefit change from your efforts in direct relationship to the community in which you reside and the availability of resources relative to your area.

Cost-Benefit Analysis

By calculating the costs of investment for specific sustainability initiatives you undertake, you can determine the payback period and savings on investment to justify the costs in the short term in relation to your cash flow. Though not as compelling as a true return on investment report, the cost-benefit analysis provides you with sufficient information for building an initial business case for new projects. Every investment made should use the format of the business case (it could be called a sustainability case) from project to project, which will clarify and justify the investments against the available capital in relation to the needs of your company and those of the community and the environment. Moreover, the cost-benefit analysis provides data and outcomes useful for marketing and transparency initiatives mentioned in the next chapter.

Return on Investment Analysis

By calculating the return on investment for the higher-impact and longer-term initiatives, you will be in a better strategic and competitive position to sustain the effort and invest in broader areas for greater return. ROI and optimization take longer and require pilot projects to gain a better view before rollout, but companies that utilize analytics to make better long-range strategic decisions will be have a tremendous advantage over those that don't. Not every investment needs to be measured by an analytics approach or have its ROI determined. This decision is based on the potential value gained by ensuring an investment that has significant cost savings is not having negative effects on productivity or the company's ability to grow. Many cost-savings initiatives harm organizations more than they realize because the results are only looked at from year to year and not with the long view.

Smart Green companies measure. Once they measure, they are ready to take their marketing and transparency plan to the next level, discussed in the following chapter.

6

Marketing Green

Next to doing the right thing, the most important thing is to let people know you are doing the right thing.

—*John D. Rockefeller*

RED-HOT GREEN

If you are successful in business, you have always known that targeting a niche and marketing and selling to that niche effectively is the key to your success. *Effectively* implies that you have grasped the needs and wants of your customers, whether it's price, quality, service, or location. It means that you have also been successful in staying ahead of your competition by being aware of changes in the marketplace. Admit it—you may be a little bit of a seer, predicting what you believe your customers will want next season. For some, you insure your investment today by creating a market that doesn't yet exist.

Billions of dollars are spent annually by companies large and small to attract customers. Spending on marketing is expected to continue to increase as the market becomes more global and the consumers more differentiated. NBC invested over $900 million to obtain the TV advertising rights to the Beijing Olympics in 2008, from which the network expected to receive a significant profit. Similarly, marketing remains a significant investment for any company.

As a business owner for over 14 years, I have spent a lot of time and money figuring out the convoluted formula for the best message, to the best audience, with the best product, at the best time. And what I've found is that effective marketing is the toughest part of the business. It's also hard to pinpoint *what* is getting the results you desire. Mine having been mostly a services-based company, I wrote a lot of articles, gave a lot of talks at conferences, and used our Web site and e-mail to cast a wide net for business. Like a Rubik's Cube, which I could never master, the best marketing formula takes research, trial and error, persistence, patience, money, and a lot of luck.

I remember early on as a start-up company developing some of the first marketing messages and graphics and thinking about wanting to be brutally honest and not presenting the company as something more than it was. This didn't mean looking cheap or just out of the garage, but rather presenting my services clearly and professionally about quality, service, and a good price.

This didn't work. I soon realized that my potential clients didn't want honesty about my abilities and services. They wanted excitement. They wanted me to be the smartest guy in the room. They wanted me to take the risks. They wanted a vision for how I was going to improve their business and help them make money. In some cases, it didn't matter that the cost was high; as long as I could demonstrate a business solution and deliver on what I promised, they would pay what was needed. So the basic axiom I learned about effective marketing is: No matter your company's size or the stage it is in, share your vision for what will benefit the client financially or nonfinancially, and deliver it well.

Evidence of the Green Rush is everywhere, which should inspire all companies to begin taking sustainability more seriously beyond seeing it as a fad for a few environmentally conscious consumers. "Green is so hot right now—both domestically and internationally—that it isn't even a movement anymore: It has become a big business with marketplace estimates ranging from $300 to $500 billion annually." The reasons? "Better consumer understanding (and scientific consensus) that the global warming phenomenon is real, escalating energy prices... and broader availability of affordable, energy-efficient products."[1]

Some rules of business never change. Whether you're selling to stakeholders inside your company or you're a budding entrepreneur pitching your case to skeptical venture capitalists, you still have to share a dream and prove you can deliver better than anyone else. Over the past few decades, though, some things have changed that add new dimensions to the Rubik's Cube of marketing your ideas that will introduce new axioms for success. The first is the rapid shift to an information-based society along with unlimited access to this information through the Internet and vast amounts of data to analyze with more powerful computing tools; and the second is the shift of awareness about the implications of climate change and diminishing resources for our near- and long-term future.

Smart Green companies with the ability to harness all three axioms effectively will stand out as victors in business. Marketing and sales are an extremely broad and complicated science that has many approaches, theories, and planning approaches that are valid; however, our discussion will be limited to the scope of concepts related to the added dimensions of greater access to information and sustainability. Many successful companies have already been catching on to these trends and are beginning to enjoy increasing market share. For example, "Procter & Gamble plans to generate at least $20 billion in cumulative sales of products with reduced environmental impact over the next five years." For sustainability marketing plans to be successful, "Actions and communications must be aligned, successful green strategies must be as sustainable as they are credible, and they must deliver sound economic ROI."[2]

FROM A NICHE MARKET TO MAINSTREAM

In this new world of up-to-the-minute information and communication, your company has already been placed on the spectrum of greenth, whether you are aware of it or not. In fact, most companies have not even begun to change internal strategies and external messages that are below the Leaf level of greenth where most consumers are beginning to pay attention. Your action (or inaction) in relation to your sustainability activities defines you. This is now an issue of competitive advantage—with pitfalls.

According to Accenture end-consumer survey on Climate Change 2007, 81 percent of citizens in the United States believe that climate change will impact their lives.[3] Most are at a very early stage of awareness and haven't begun making conscious decisions about their actions, but thanks to the increase in the price of oil and the subsequent escalation of the prices of everything else, the average consumer is increasingly changing his or her buying habits based on new criteria that the person may not have even labeled yet: green.

"Becoming sustainable is trendy these days, so it is not too difficult to get people on the program," says Mark Estill of Piedmont Biofuels Industrial LLC. "Biodiesel has become a viable alternative as we see an increase in petroleum prices. This is a method to replace diesel with something more environmentally-friendly. We anticipate a trend and make some cash at the same time."

The home building industry has seen a lot of change and growth toward green. With buildings and homes being responsible for over half of the harmful emissions and waste that contributes to global warming, the entire industry is trying to redefine itself during the Green Rush. Chad Ray of Old Heritage Builders, who started building green homes several years ago, has seen the trend evolve over time with his clients: "It's been interesting. Nothing happens overnight. We are in our fourth or fifth year of incorporating new things into our business model. We didn't try to overwhelm anyone. We took a small, incremental approach. Once they know something is genuinely important to you they will take notice. People are scared of things they are not comfortable with. We still put out a new thing or two that we want to try."

Before the media explosion and the recent Green Rush, Ed Barr, a green developer, saw a small niche grow significantly in just the past 18 months: "Prior to that there has always been an interested clientele in our niche market. That niche market is now becoming more mainstream." The executive director of the NC-based Green Home Council in North Carolina, Bill Beasley, continues to educate consumers and builders as the trend toward green continues to rise: "Being a band of volunteers, we have excellent commitment and buy-in from within our organization. Our customers [builders and developers] are showing increasing interest. In general, our challenge is to demonstrate to our customers that running a sustainable business and building sustainable homes is in everyone's best interest."

For some, the change can't happen quickly enough. Consumers may be contemplating action but are still checking their wallets. "Customers really like the idea of the product or system," says one building retailer, "but not as many of them are putting their money where their mouth is yet. Some are sold on the idea, and that is where they are going. [As to] the idea of a whole systems approach to sustainability, we as a society are not there yet. It's not a quick sell." But depending on the product, customers may clamor to buy your product; such an example is rain catchment technology: "We have a huge buy-in from consumers, almost completely. Customers clearly are looking for my product. I don't have to find clients—they find me."

When it comes to energy, the vice president of operations of Advanced Energy observes that cost may still be a factor inhibiting complete buy-in. "Lots of people want to get on the green band-wagon. Genuine interest is there, but people pause when it comes to the cost of implementation. We're working hard to figure out how to make it easier for customers to implement energy-efficient technology without breaking their budget."

THE GREEN CONSUMER

Who are the green consumers? Actually, we all are. Just as companies can't escape the scrutiny of an increasingly discriminating consumer, consumers are under the scrutiny of each other as a community in transition, looking for new meaning in their purchasing power and the desire to make a difference in the world or their health. The segmentation of green consumers can become convoluted: "There are true-blue greens, green-back greens, sprouts and grousers. There are optimists, people of faith, pragmatics, cynics and pessimists with entirely divergent views on saving the planet." Some are radical and progressive when it comes to the environment and society, while others are more interested in personal health, wellness, and a toxin-free home.[4]

Attitudes and beliefs about green consumers and what demographics they represent have been increasing at an accelerating rate. Many are reaching the same conclusion about the basic traits of a green consumer as succinctly summarized by BSDglobal. com: Green consumers are sincere in their intentions, judge their personal actions as environmentally inadequate, don't consider companies to be perfect but they should be taking steps to improve, they may overstate how green they really are, don't want a quick fix but are generally unwilling to make huge sacrifices, they distrust company green reports and claims unless verified by a third party, they lack basic knowledge about green issues but are eager to learn, and the most responsive group are young adults and the least responsive are those born before 1950.[5] Changes in green consumer behavior are occurring more and more as each year passes with more information becoming available and more easily accessible.

What are green consumers looking for? "Consumers are looking for companies to educate them." They have grown up with certain brands they trust, but now they are open to something new. These new green consumers will financially reward companies that are more socially responsible and environmentally progressive in their actions. Amy Hall, director of social consciousness for women's clothing company Eileen Fisher, stated, "It's always been our belief that if we do the right thing for the people and the product, the profit will follow."[6]

Tempered by the inaction of still a very large number of consumers, not everyone is necessarily buying into green even if they believe it to be important. Joel Makower, journalist and editor of the *Green Business Newsletter* and a key member of the board for Greenbiz.com, asserted that many consumers just aren't up to speed on all of the issues related to green. Why? "(1) There's no mandate. Consumers will still go for a cheaper product if it's convenient and they recognize the brand. [It's a] tough sell to send them to new products that cost more and are at different retail locations. (2) The public is dazed and confused," without clear, centralized messages about what is green and what is the scientific basis. There is still no clear consensus on what is best for the environment. "(3) People lack perspective." With the flurry of green messages and images in the marketplace, it's becoming increasingly difficult for customers to discern what is imitating green and what is really green. "(4) Companies making greener products are afraid to speak up." By tooting their horn prematurely or without regard to a more systems-based approach to the impact of their products, some companies erred and were punished for their mistake. They aren't ready to make the same mistake again, so are keeping claims about their products' benefits to a minimum. "(5) Green benefits aren't always evident. Many companies making a huge difference in their energy conservation efforts and reduction or change in their materials are too abstract for most consumers to appreciate."

The Shelton Group, a marketing research firm, released a study entitled "Eco Pulse," which polled more than 3.5 million people to understand the best marketing approaches for green companies. "When asked if personal comfort, convenience, or the environment took priority, only 31 percent of respondents chose the environment."[7] Many consumers are feeling green fatigue, which results in the buying levels of green products not being as high as many companies were hoping for.

However, the Green Rush is in full swing and consumers are becoming wiser. There are many new segments in the marketplace emerging that are influencing many others. Even articles that continue to bash the sustainability movement as a trendy fad that will pass away once the price of gas dips below $3 per gallon (is that cheap?) will be drowned out by the increase in information shared across new media outlets such as social networks and blogs.

At this point, the tipping point has already occurred; businesses need to address the issues from a strategic planning and marketing perspective—if not today, then very soon. Obviously, companies need to address the issues of greenwashing, and jumping the gun with messages that don't match their reality behind closed doors. This will quickly come back to bite them and harm other legitimate sustainability efforts within their sector. There is a big difference, though, between forcefully communicating your vision and trying to convince your customer that you are greener than your competitor. Jonathan Tannenbaum in "Will Green Marketing Bring You the Green?" asserts through interviews with other companies that "corporate marketing strategies need to go beyond green for green's sake." Marketing effectiveness is going to be dependent on four basic approaches: (1) Keep the message simple: What is this doing for me? (2) Speak specifically about issues the consumer understands. (3) Don't place the blame for global warming on the consumer's behavior as part of your message. (4) Focus on how this will help the consumer's family and secondarily the world.

Just as rapidly as a product hits the market with great promise of being green, that same product can go stale on the shelves because of the speed of access to information and the ability to share it with others through one of the most powerful marketing tools to come out since the television—social networks.

My four children, ages 28, 23, 18, and 16, have grown up accustomed to Internet communications, beginning with chat and e-mail. Now they have hundreds of "friends" in their social networks (Facebook and MySpace), and each of these friends has similar-sized links. My 18-year-old son hears a new indie band and sends a post on Facebook to 1,200 friends to give it a listen. That virally spreads to tens if not hundreds of thousands of other friends within a few days. YouTube videos likewise are being used to virally transmit powerful messages and events that stir up interest and/or controversy. Up until recently, social networks were seen as the domain of teens and college students, but now more savvy businesspeople are signing in. One college student I overheard saying that her professor announced he had opened a Facebook account. Her response to this was, "Ew, you're too old." He was 44.

So now a great new leveler of the playing field is in the mix. There is now more and better information available with a fast, viral delivery system in place connected to computers and smartphones. Every company, no matter its size, sector, or status, needs to be considering this new marketplace and the means to communicate its message within it.

So how do Smart Green companies think about their market? And what do green consumers want? In a nutshell, they want it all, whether they are completely informed about all the issues or not: green products, sustainable companies, and better health for themselves and for the planet. They want responsible companies providing responsible products at an affordable price. It used to be quality, on-time, best price. Now it's quality, on-time, affordable price (traded fairly), and limited impact on the environment from its creation to its disposal or reuse. But saving the environment is not the only reason consumers are seeking out companies and products that are more sustainable.

Laurie Demeritt, president and COO of the Hartman Group, a sustainability marketing research firm, stated: "We have noticed a growth in our business about 8 to 10 years ago due to the health and wellness movement more than anything. The consumer sustainability actions are largely health motivated—not from a desire to protect the environment. Organic food is a gateway for many consumers. They choose foods that are healthy for them (self-motivated product selection). Consumers are also starting to buy water and air filtration (again due to the potential health benefits). Consumers are pragmatic in what they are doing to make changes, not necessarily thinking of their carbon footprint yet. The water bottle is a good example. Some people think that consumers are trying to reduce their waste by carrying their own water bottle, but really they are worried about their health—the plastic leaching toxins into the water of disposable bottles."

Solar Solutions notices a change in perception among consumers about the payback period for investing in green solutions: "We are seeing a rising interest in sustainability, so there is a rising interest in solar power. But the cost is still too high for solar power versus electricity in this state [so] it's been a hard sell from the sustainability angle until now."

Zely and Ritz, on the other hand, is a restaurant in Raleigh, North Carolina that sources virtually all of its ingredients from local, organic farms. The owners know each farmer by first name and precisely where each ingredient comes from. The chef says, "When you eat ingredients that are grown locally and in season they taste better. We have more customers who are interested in supporting local farmers. The sustainability of local farms is really important."

Smart Green companies pay attention to the trends of increased knowledge of their consumers, understand their desire to learn more and to be more responsible to the environment and to the community, and take the time to learn for themselves those activities that are achievable and that match their level of greenth, preventing many of the pitfalls of appearing to be greenwashing. Consumers want to know more about how products are made, where the materials come from, and how they were transported. They want a story that is positive, believable, and easy to understand. One company executive realized "[we] needed to make our products visible: Sometimes people say, 'Wow, I didn't know you had this product,' and that is nice. The biggest factor is raising awareness in consumers as to the products available." Once consumers can understand and accept your story and continue to grow with your growth, there is a higher chance of success.

The key factor in preparing for a sustainability marketing plan is to reassess the basic building blocks of what motivates consumers to buy one product over another in the context of sustainable outcomes. As one marketing research firm describes it, "To succeed, eco-entrepreneurs must not neglect the traditional values of price, quality, convenience, and availability." When it comes to price, consumers will usually pay up to 2 percent more if they believe they are getting more value. Consumers are prejudiced about the quality of green products, like for example a bathroom cleaner that doesn't smell like pine, lemon, or ammonia but it gets the job done just as well. Quality must be communicated and demonstrated very clearly, usually tested by performance, appearance, subjective feelings, and durability. Convenience is critical, because consumers don't want to be put out to buy something different, even it's better. They will give up if products are not convenient and available in a reasonable fashion.

As mentioned before, one of the pitfalls in trying to gain competitive advantage too early or outside your level of greenth is greenwashing. *Greenwashing* is a term used to describe "the act of misleading consumers regarding the environmental practices of a company or the environmental benefits of a product or service," according to TerraChoice Environmental Marketing.[8]

"The Six Sins of Greenwashing" listed by TerraChoice are becoming more prevalent as the competition for consumer loyalty for green products increases. The first mistake is to have a hidden trade-off; you don't recognize that one environmental issue is a problem, such as shipping an organic product from halfway around the world to your table. The second mistake is when a company has no proof of its products being green; it has no certifications or third-party verifications. Third, companies that perpetuate vague or overgeneralized claims about their green products render their message meaningless; calling something "green," "eco," "natural," or "earth-friendly" increases suspicion. Fourth is sharing irrelevant information that has nothing to do with the product being environmentally sustainable. Fifth, outright lying about a product's properties and certifications for being green may capture consumers' attention until they look up your certification verification on publicly available Web sites and your product is toast, not to mention your own liability for fraudulent behavior. Finally, when a company is marketing the lesser of two evils, such as lemon-scented ammonia that smells earth-friendly or less harmful pesticides and herbicides, it may be a sign for *consumers* to change their buying decisions.

With the Internet now as powerful a marketing tool as any other medium, if not more so, the benefits and risks of viral marketing need to be mentioned. First of all, before launching any campaign through social networks and blogs, which can be very effective in creating buzz about your product, be aware that it requires constant maintenance and vigilance to keep your true vision and mission in the forefront. If another blogger calls you on possible greenwashing, it could ultimately lead to a very large, negative messaging campaign that can damage your effort. On the Internet, you can't sit back and let things remain without a fight. If the accusation is true, it's better to come clean and talk about the steps you will take in order to address the issue. Honesty is usually accepted and appreciated by a normally cynical crowd.

Read and listen to your customers' comments. There is a lot to learn in their blogs that can help guide your own messages. Consumers are not just looking for green products; they are looking for value for their dollar, which happens to include social equity issues and environmental stewardship in addition to the product benefits. And finally, choose the issues you plan to take on very carefully; it doesn't have to be every issue.

Your knowledge and study of the issues in your preparation for strategic sustainability planning help you narrow the issues to those that matter most for your product sales.

DEVELOPING YOUR SMART GREEN MARKETING PLAN

Unique to developing a Smart Green marketing plan are three key stages of planning: (1) Conduct market research on the competitive elements of your product. (2) Take extra care and time to unpack as many of the beneficial aspects of the product as possible in relation to the environment and to the betterment of the community. (3) Quantify those benefits in both financial and nonfinancial metrics.

Some companies have found new insights about their products that have made all the difference in their marketing and sales efforts. Don't be afraid to think outside the box and to be open to reassessing the nature of your product and how it can evolve into something even better over time with more research and development.

Align your Smart Green marketing plan with your sustainability strategic plan. Like the steps leading up to developing your sustainability strategic plan, your Smart Green marketing plan should follow a pattern of research from your community and consumers. Furthermore, you need to determine your level of greenth, establish your mission and goals, develop a plan, implement a pilot program, measure the outcomes for business value, and roll out the full marketing plan based on the successful outcomes of the pilot. The best marketing plans are detailed and highly substantiated with data about consumers, markets, pricing, and product benefits, with the additional components that define the green benefits consumers respond to best.

Deliver your Smart Green marketing plan with as many tools and media as possible to reach as many differentiated audiences in the most economical means. For example, BDG Marketing suggests, "Selling and promotional tools, targeted media, direct marketing, trade shows, Web and interactive messaging, and a host of other marketing tactics are all part of a company's arsenal for effective delivery of its green message." I would add social networks such as Facebook, Plaxo, LinkedIn, and MySpace; chat networks such as Twitter; bookmark sites such as Diggit; and blogs as additional, specific tools available.

Manage your environmental message by establishing support (action and capital) from all necessary stakeholders on how the image is to be presented and maintained. Obtain the same support across the enterprise by establishing internal Smart Green action committees for education, assessment, and monitoring of trends of consumers and the industry for the organization. Establish a center of expertise within the environmental and social aspects, cradle-to-cradle product life cycle, and other benefits of your product that will have customers and partners coming to you for education and advice.

Establish a change plan for your products that enables your company to assess the environmental impact of each product, your company's operations, and those of your partners and vendors. Establish a long-term goal with a budget and design considerations in relation to possible competitive companies garnering consumer support for their products as well as cost savings to your organization. Make sure your product improvements are in line with and if possible exceed consumer expectations.

Continuously research and assess the environmental attitudes and purchasing behavior of your consumers. Form public/private partnerships with those organizations that can best enhance your company's success and knowledge about your environmental impacts. Understate your environmental messages to stay on the safe side of consumer perception that companies are generally not to be believed when disclosing these types of messages. Whenever possible, let others praise your efforts. Be quick to admit to errors and be open to suggestions for possible changes in your goals and practices. Become an expert in communicating your environmental messages and benefits in layman's terms.

Focus your marketing campaign more heavily on public relations (PR) than on advertising. Form connections with community outreach entities, chambers of commerce, service organizations, and the public to learn about serving the community better as a business partner in a regional approach. Educate other companies, organizations, and partners. Be prepared for bad press and utilize talented, technically minded people in addition to PR professionals.

When developing an advertising campaign, provide consumers with simple but sufficient information so that they can make their own judgment about your claims. Avoid ads that simply indicate your interest in the environment with mountains, streams, and butterflies. Test ads with focus groups of green consumers before they are deployed. Seek third-party content as much as possible for your print ads. Carefully get the support of young people to help promote the product to their parents or to the public. Highlight novel aspects of your product, like the packaging, but don't overdo it. Use a variety of marketing strategies, such as more detailed information in the form of brochures, videos, YouTube video blogs, consumer hotlines for responses to questions about products, classroom curricula, magazine articles, community meetings, and online Webinars.

Research and begin to fulfill requirements for certifications that will increase your transparency and demonstrate your efforts and results as acknowledged by a third party. *Transparency* is the term to describe the degree by which a company discloses its data to the public, including environmental and social impacts. Certifications are a shorthand means to increase transparency, but there have been calls from consumers to increase disclosure even further. Companies are beginning to be rewarded as they increase their transparency. Certifications for making green claims began over 25 years ago, and by the early 1990s nearly 13 percent of new products had some form of green claim. Today there are many certifications across every sector.

You must choose the certifications wisely for budgetary reasons, credibility, and bang for the buck to invest in one. Certifications provide a useful shorthand for consumers to investigate whether they trust a product and company. Here are brief descriptions of some of the current, well-respected certifications for products, taken from the BSDglobal.com Web site:[9]

- *Scientific Certification Systems (SCS)* of Oakland, California, was founded in 1984 to measure pesticide residues in agricultural products. It now certifies a wide array of environmental and food safety claims. Under its Environmental Claims Certification Program, introduced in 1990, SCS has certified single-criteria claims such as "recycled content," "biodegradable," "water-efficient," and "no VOCs" [volatile organic compounds] for more than 1,100 products.

- *Green Seal* is a U.S.-based, nonprofit environmental labeling organization that awards a seal of approval to products that are found to cause significantly less harm to the environment than other similar products. Green Seal develops environmental standards for consumer products through a public review process involving manufacturers, environmentalists, consumers, and government agencies. Green Seal has developed standards for more than 50 product categories, including paints, household cleaners, paper products, water-efficient fixtures, lighting, windows, and major household appliances.

- Canada's government-sponsored *Environmental Choice* program started by evaluating single-criterion product claims, but has subsequently adopted a life-cycle review process. Certified items carry the EcoLogo—three doves intertwined to form the shape of a maple leaf.

Other important certifications are:

- *The Global Reporting Initiative (GRI)* based in the Netherlands has pioneered the development of the world's most widely used sustainability reporting framework and is committed to its continuous improvement and application worldwide. Mostly deployed in Europe and gaining new ground in the United States and other parts of the world, this framework sets out the principles and indicators that organizations can use to measure and report their economic, environmental, and social performance. The cornerstone of the framework is the Sustainability Reporting Guidelines. The third version of the Guidelines— known as the G3 Guidelines—was published in 2006, and is free to the public. Other components of the framework include Sector Supplements (unique indicators for industry sectors), Protocols (detailed reporting guidance), and National Annexes (unique country-level information). Sustainability reports based on the GRI framework can be used to benchmark organizational performance with respect to laws, norms, codes, performance standards, and voluntary initiatives; demonstrate organizational commitment to sustainable development; and compare organizational performance over time. GRI promotes and develops this standardized approach to reporting to stimulate demand for sustainability information—which will benefit reporting organizations and those who use report information alike.

- *The ISO 14000* family addresses various aspects of environmental management. The intention of ISO 14001:2004 is to provide a framework for a holistic, strategic approach to the organization's environmental policy, plans, and actions that has the effect of establishing a common reference for communicating about environmental management issues between organizations and their customers, regulators, the public, and other stakeholders. Because ISO 14001:2004 does not lay down levels of environmental performance, the standard can be implemented by a wide variety of organizations, whatever their current level of environmental maturity. However, a commitment to compliance with applicable environmental legislation and regulations is required, along with a commitment to continual improvement.

Smart Green companies have a dual challenge before them when it comes to marketing because of the cost of researching, developing, and maintaining a meaningful message directed to an intensively scrutinizing and highly cynical audience while at the same time trying to implement and manage their sustainability initiatives without greenwashing. It should get easier, but more standards and guides are needed for companies to effectively communicate their messages without all the burden of costly and mismatched data and outcomes to live up to consumer expectations. For now, the best approach is to dive in, share your vision with a passion, be willing to take criticism, be open to change, and keep your eye on the ball for what best communicates your message to your customers.

7

Building Smart Green Companies

A business that makes nothing but
money is a poor business.

—Henry Ford

DEMONSTRATING BUSINESS VALUE

Smart Green companies are those that strive to incorporate meaning, purpose, and the systems view of their impact. Meanwhile, they must also continuously demonstrate business value to their customers and other stakeholders by applying the critical success factors of vision, talent, capital, and caring to the everyday concerns of running an enterprise with all the challenges and frustrations that are intrinsic to business. As most entrepreneurs know, the best-laid plans will not always succeed the way that you expect them to, but the ups and downs of business can open new doors that weren't noticeable before.

After almost nine years of running my company, my transition out as CEO was facilitated by my investment board, who felt it was time the company would be better led by a veteran executive than the founder. These transitions occur frequently in business, especially if the scales of ownership are tipped over time as more capital is raised to fuel the vision.

Though the break was painful and disappointing, I soon realized that as an entrepreneur I could start over and apply my skills and experience to a new vision.

I partnered with Zemo Trevathan, one of my previous investors, and we started a company, Strategic Measures, Inc., which expanded on the idea of measuring the business impact of training to include all other cost centers within the organization. Most of the interest came from a department within many large corporations that had been relegated to the bottom of the line-item budget and the top of the list for annual budget cuts when times got tough: facilities management. Facilities managers were becoming leaders in some of the companies' first efforts to go green with actions such as saving energy and water and becoming LEED certified. The key issue that facilities managers had difficulty with was proving the business value they knew was real but couldn't demonstrate and communicate effectively to corporate stakeholders.

Business value can be defined as the financial contribution of an individual or team that is measured as a return on investment (ROI) and that achieves the strategic goals of the organization. Demonstrating and communicating business value are critical to companies incorporating sustainability principles into their planning, because business value, both actual and perceived, is the justification and motivation needed by all stakeholders to keep a vision alive. This could mean changes in budget, investment, personnel, or products and services—no matter how talented, important, or well-meaning they are.

As budgets become tighter in a fluctuating economy, companies are forced to cut costs, close factories, reduce head count, and all other means to weather the storm. Business managers and entrepreneurs have to make these kinds of tough decisions frequently, and the role of a facilities manager, information technology (IT) manager, training manager, or other leader in a cost center as a business value analyst is more important than ever.

As entrepreneurs start new companies built upon principles of sustainability and existing companies begin changing their corporate culture, products, and facilities to a sustainable model, they have to become more actively aware of the concept of business value. Managers within the most successful companies will be able to be clear about what encourages and destroys business value, identify and measure key metrics for business value, understand the implications of real versus perceived value, and translate their budget line items into a business case.

HOW DO YOU CREATE OR DESTROY BUSINESS VALUE?

Members of a facilities management team explored how they currently create and destroy value. The open-ended questions in Table 7.1 helped to facilitate a more open and honest analysis of how corporate policies and culture impact business value.

Starting a green company does not make you immune to the pitfalls of destroying value. A biofuels company in eastern North Carolina hoped to become the largest producer of biofuels in the

Table 7.1   Creating/Destroying Business Value

How do you create value?	How do you destroy value?
Adding (actionable) knowledge, not information	Not having a clear definition of value
Increase profit through sales	Not being able to communicate our value effectively
Communicating effectively	
Continuity of supply	Focus on quality as an expertise
Analyzing possible solutions	Lose sales
Ensuring regulatory compliance	Duplication of roles and tasks
Quantifying risk	Loss of reputation
Providing information and feedback about the effectiveness/impact of training	Bureaucracy
	Inappropriate use of funds
	Not seeing the big picture—silos
Find out from clients how they create value	Taking short-term shortcuts
	Measurement not connected to value
Maximizing the performance of my employees	Meeting "metrics" as opposed to value
Align my objectives with business objectives	In general, proceeding without reflecting on value creation (even when things are going well)
Selling products and services	
Staying current with processes and procedures	

Southeast, only to lose its way in a scandal involving bribes to a congressman when investment capital came up short. Even a company with the potential to provide a great sustainability model for the region can fall prey to a lack of integrity.

HOW DO CORPORATE FINANCIAL GOALS IMPEDE YOUR VALUE CREATION?

The facilities management team also explored how the current corporate culture of cost containment affects their department and ultimately the company as a whole by listing those attitudes and actions stakeholders take, revealing a disconnect between department knowledge and corporate decisions:

- Corporate goals are shortsighted—one year is not enough time for proving ROI.

- Facilities management value contribution is not fully recognized.

- Corporate values are not aligned with departmental values.

- Stakeholders don't recognize our expertise for analysis.

Since most budgets are managed by the chief financial officer and the accounting department, cost centers are often the victim of the 10 percent rule: If they saved us 10 percent last year, they can save us 10 percent this year. The focus on cost savings, a necessary step in stabilizing a company during difficult times, can't be repeated year to year without considering the value each cost center contributes to the competitive value of the organization. I have seen blind cost cuts undermine the morale of an organization, resulting in the loss of some of its best talent.

Sometimes, by cutting costs from easy targets that can't show compelling financial outcomes like widgets produced or widgets sold, such as facilities management, IT, and human resources, they inadvertently lose out on greater value (revenue) for the company that could be gained with more strategic spending. The responsibility for demonstrating and communicating this value resides with the department head, who needs to identify and measure the best metrics in the form of a business case.

WHAT METRICS DO YOU USE AND HOW DO YOU MEASURE BUSINESS VALUE?

As companies and departments begin to include sustainability metrics, business value will become increasingly difficult to measure and demonstrate—all the more reason to explore what are the most important metrics and methodology for measurement as part of the planning process. Table 7.2 lists examples of metrics the facilities management team considers to be most important.

Choosing the right metrics and using the appropriate tools for measurement are critical for establishing value within your company or department. An IT department in a prestigious bank realized

Table 7.2   How Do You Measure Your Business Value?

On-time completion of projects	Audit results
No significant regulatory events	Number of complaints
Customer surveys	Where/type of complaint source
360° feedbacks	Track past preventive actions and
On budget	their impact
Key Performance Indicators (KPI's)	Baseline/look for trends
Lines of backorders	Frequency/repeats
Stock price	Follow up measurements on usage
Repeat customers	Degree of being in line with
# of detained or held shipments	corporate objectives
Metrics on time/process and	Data showing $ impact of on-time
regulations	delivery
	Research (other companies)
	Cost of being late (opportunity cost)

its existence was in jeopardy as more internal departments began outsourcing the same services the IT department was providing. Value was being determined by the number of trouble tickets being generated each month, which affected the budgetary allocations to the department. Slowly sinking under a pile of trouble tickets and being cut out of new equipment, full-time employees, and new internal contracts, the department needed to recalibrate its value. By shifting the focus to the value of uptime in a banking environment at 99.8 percent over 10 years, the department could pit itself against its competition, which was unwilling to guarantee such stellar metrics. New investment for the department provided faster, more reliable servers, better-trained technicians, and better productivity software, reducing the number of trouble tickets and increasing the value of the department to the bottom line of the company.

A sustainability initiative will suffer the same scrutiny following the glowing report of cost savings in the first year and end up being a potential drain on the organization if it can't demonstrate ongoing, meaningful value. Choosing the right metrics, linking them to the goals and strategies of the organization, and measuring the business impact will provide the necessary information for the business case to maintain the sustainability efforts or to let those go who are not generating the level of value expected. As the data indicating social and environmental impact becomes more widely available and reliable, the relationships between moving from one level of greenth to another, for example, can be better monitored and justified to stakeholders.

HOW DO YOU MANAGE PERCEPTIONS OF BUSINESS VALUE?

Equally valuable to managing the actual outcomes of business value is the management of perceptions of value. Many managers and business owners trying to communicate their value, even in the form of a business case, find it difficult to convince stakeholders of the value. This is mainly due to a difference of perception. Your stakeholders may be at a lower level of greenth and cannot yet fully appreciate or see the value of your green initiatives. The facilities team working on their business value assessment completed a grid illustrated in Table 7.3 that indicates their own perceptions of value for projects juxtaposed with those of their stakeholders.

Perceptions of value may change from year to year depending on the priorities of the company and the degree of external social and economic forces impacting the company. In one instance, a company decided to cut back on its facilities budget by changing to a less expensive food provider and reducing the number of times the floors were vacuumed, windows cleaned, and lawns mowed. The perception from management was that in decreasing the frequency of these cosmetic tasks, the savings would outweigh other considerations. In fact, employees noticed and educated management that these cosmetic tasks were part of their reason for remaining with the company. For many employees, the building's appearance and amenities represented the quality and prestige of what they wanted for themselves. Many alumni from universities who contribute money indicate the reason as "the beauty of the campus" rather than "academic prestige." Management reinstated the food service and restored the frequency of the cleaning tasks.

Table 7.3 Perceptions of Business Value (Seminar Examples)

Activity	Positive Perception of Value	Negative Perception of Value	Not Applicable
Data Management System	FM Team	Management	Employees
Rapid Order Fulfillment	Management	FM Team	Employees
100% Accuracy	Management	FM Team	Employees
New Product Launches	Management		FM Team Employees
Employee Safety	Management Employees FM Team		
Group Forums	FM Team	Management	Employees
Increasing Benefits	Employees FM Team	Management	
Better In-house Food	Employees	Management	FM Team

Managing perceptions in relation to sustainability will be equally important. In fact, many new, talented employees are choosing a company to work for and remain with in terms of its sustainability strategy in addition to pay scale, mobility, and benefits. Green consumers may choose products in part because of what's on the label of the product, but increasingly they are becoming more concerned about the supply chain above and below the product: where and how it was made and where it goes after it's used. Many companies that do not manage perceptions as well as actual benefits could find themselves losing both employees and customers.

Many of the executives I interviewed described their companies' value in a variety of ways, but they continue to explore how to describe their value to customers and stakeholders in ways that are consistent with their sustainability vision. Since there are no criteria or standards for what is right in sustainability, entrepreneurs have the freedom to test their beliefs in the open marketplace, some with better results than others.

With no clear definition of sustainability, Nancy Murray of Builders of Hope in Raleigh, North Carolina, confidently asserts, "We are changing the face of affordable housing. The affordable housing crisis is everywhere—and we don't just need affordable housing, but workforce housing for teachers and police officers. Over half of all teachers in Raleigh live outside of the district where they teach. The development of entire neighborhoods based upon a model of recycling old homes slated for demolition, incorporating green standards, and new job opportunities for at-risk individuals, with homes made available to families of below median income—that serves the ideals of both environmental and social consciousness."

The owner of Solar Solutions is still waiting for the market to mature for the value of his product to be realized so the perceived value of his products can shift from being too expensive to being a justifiable cost. Many consumers are still measuring their support of green products and sustainability against the payback period, like the cost of a new economy car against the cost differential of the price of gas over time. He said, "I don't have a definition for sustainability at this point. Electricity is so cheap in our state, so I have not really pushed the sustainability aspect. At this time, it takes too long to recoup the cost of the product. Even with the rising interest in sustainability and the obvious rising interest in solar power, the cost is still too high for solar power versus electricity. It's a hard sell from the sustainability angle."

Some business owners, like James O'Mara, owner of a landscaping company in Chapel Hill, North Carolina, have the desire to change but are just trying to keep the doors open. When I spoke to him about what he thought about sustainability and how he might shift toward going green, he responded, "Show me the products. There aren't any that I would be able to use yet. I want to change because I know that going green is important, but what is more important to me right now is staying open for business. We are still in the worst season of drought in 50 years, gas is $4 per gallon, half of my best workers returned home to Mexico to get their papers updated and now can't get back into the country without crossing illegally, and my landscaping business has slowed down because of the housing crunch." What James is experiencing is typical with any business facing the harsh realities of meeting financial challenges, weather problems, labor shortages, and a dearth of alternative products to choose from.

BECOMING A SMART GREEN COMPANY

In addition to the opportunities in a burgeoning green market and in spite of the hardships and pitfalls in overcoming the disparity between actual and perceived value of your business or project, what does it take to become a Smart Green company? Does the sector you're in affect your success? Some making the effort are eco-entrepreneurs, launching new companies with a focus on taking advantage of the Green Rush and striving to incorporate sustainability principles in their everyday operations. Others are existing companies trying to make a change toward their principles of what sustainability means to them.

The steps for preparing to either launch a new green company or start a new sustainability initiative within your organization have already been outlined. The creation and evolution of a Smart Green company can best be illustrated by showing an example of an actual company and its journey toward change.

SMART GREEN PROFILE: THE GENERAL STORE CAFÉ

Description

The General Store Café in Pittsboro, North Carolina, recently won the prestigious award of being "Best Restaurant in the Triangle" in a local magazine. The Café has not only become a favorite hangout for locals in Chatham County, but it has also attracted the attention of diners from throughout the Research Triangle. The Café has become a community center by supporting local artists, musicians, and nonprofits. Three nights a week, local musicians play, and every first Monday of the month the café hosts a Burrito Bash to help raise money for local nonprofits. Recently expanded with a larger stage, bar, kitchen, and dining area, the Café is prepared to continue its community center tradition for many years to come.

Level of Greenth Analysis

From the outset, the General Store Café had a vision of sustainability. Early on, the owners secured local sources for the Café's produce in order to cater to the growing community of green-conscious diners by offering organic foods, fair-trade coffees, and hormone-free meats in the menu. To increase traffic to the Café, artists were invited to display their works, musicians were invited to play and sell their music, and nonprofits could sign up to receive proceeds from a Monday night Burrito Bash when the Café donates all sales of burrito dishes to a selected local nonprofit organization. Given its stage of development and the progress the Café has made with its recent expansion and its plans for the future, the Café's level of greenth is a Twig, as illustrated in Table 7.4.

Analysis of Company Biosphere

The General Store Café is located in the center of Pittsboro, the county seat, in the heart of Chatham County, one of the fastest-growing counties in North Carolina. Residents of Pittsboro are a diverse group of artists and farmers, merchants and students, and the town supports software developers, biofuel research and production, antique shops, and art galleries (from the Town of Pittsboro Web site: www.pittsboronc.org). Table 7.5 expands on the regional biosphere for Chatham County to provide context and awareness of the community, economics, and environment the business is in, and Table 7.6 expands on the company biosphere for benchmarking and planning.

Sustainability Mission Statement

Chatham County is on the brink of rapid growth, and the General Store Café is ready to grow with it. The Café tripled its size while still retaining the cozy atmosphere of the cafe's original space and adding other intimate restaurant sections.

Table 7.4 Level of Greenth Customized for The General Store Café, Pittsboro, NC

Sample Activities	Level I	Level II (Goals)
Organizational Structure	Hierarchical with a consortium of local shareholders.	Increase shareholder base with opportunities for employee ownership based on tenure.
Employee Relations	Increase diversity at least by 25%, livable wage, basic bonus structure.	
Strategic Plan	Mission Statement includes commitment to sustainability.	Need to develop comprehensive Sustainability Strategic Plan for three years and connect investments to business outcomes.
Carbon Footprint	Some Energy Conservation.	Need to measure footprint and implement additional activities for energy conservation and alternative forms of energy use.
Community Service	Public/Private Partnerships, Donations, Board Membership.	Owner/Operator is a board member on the local Arts Council, participates in local fundraisers and festivals, donates to local charities, supports the local artists and musicians.

Water Usage	Some Water Conservation.	Water catchment design on roof is in place. Conversation effort underway.
Product Lifecycle	50% of products from vendors and suppliers represent sustainable model (local, organic, energy efficient, fair).	Need to measure footprint and implement additional activities for energy conservation and alternative forms of energy use.
Measurement Approach	Cost/Benefit analysis based on budget.	Plan for C/B Analysis being developed to determine return on investment.
Marketing	Mission statement made public on the website and on the menu. Flyer with more information available when requested.	All product sources and suppliers are disclosed on the menu, on the website, and in tbhe Café. Plan for transparency report being developed.
Waste	Reduced waste by 25% in current.	Reduction of waste by 75% in 3 years.

Table 7.5 Sample Categories of Regional Biosphere Analysis

Regional Biosphere Analysis Categories	Customized Information
Regional Awareness	Population Growth Rate Median Age The tax rate Transportation Policy Initiatives
Energy Awareness	Energy Sources Energy Usage Energy Impacts Energy Initiatives Alternative Fuels Policy Initiatives
Social Awareness	Cultural Diversity Literacy Rates Changes in Income Crime Rates Employment Health Education Birth/Death Rates Graduation Rates Higher Education Policy Initiatives
Bio Awareness	Climate Waterways Major Landforms Weather Patterns Flora and Fauna Agricultural Zone Groundwater Sources and Levels Waste Methods Waste Impacts Waste Altenatives Air Quality CO_2 Emissions Other Emissions Water Quality Policy Initiatives

Table 7.6   Sample Company Biosphere Analysis Categories

Company Biosphere Analysis Categories	
Footprint Analysis	Energy Sources
	Energy Usage
	Energy Impacts
	Energy Initiatives
	Alternative Fuels
	Waste Methods
	Waste Impacts
	Waste Alternatives
	Air Quality
	CO2 Emissions
	Other Emissions
	Water Sources
	Water Quality
Product Life Cycle Analysis	Food
	Origin
	Sources
	Delivery
	Distributor
	Consumption
	Waste/Reuse
	Supplies
	Origin
	Sources
	Delivery
	Distributor
	Consumption
	Waste/Reuse
	Equipment
	Origin
	Sources
	Delivery
	Distributor
	Consumption
	Waste/Reuse

(continued)

Table 7.6 (*continued*)

Company Biosphere Analysis
Categories

Business and Community Relationship Analysis	Business Relationships
	Food
	Cost Breaks
	Terms
	Alt Sources and Terms
	Supplies
	Cost Breaks
	Terms
	Alt Sources and Terms
	Equipment
	Cost Breaks
	Terms
	Alt Sources and Terms
	Services
	Cost Breaks
	Terms
	Alt Sources and Terms
Cashflow Analysis	Annual Revenue Profit and Loss
	Income
	Black Bird Bar
	Restaurant
	Catering
	Other Income
	Expenses
	COGS
	Overhead
	Balance

Table 7.7   Product Sustainability Plan

Sustainability Initiative	Description	Estimated Cost	Estimated Benefit
Local Sourcing	Food Supplies Equipment Services		
Energy Reduction			
Energy Diversification			
Water Reduction			
Community Support			
ROI to Investors	Provide an opportunity for local patrons to become part of the investment community	Legal fees:	8% per annum

Table 7.8   Sustainability Marketing Plan

Business Activity
Restaurant
Black Bird Bar
Catering
Events Planning

The sustainability mission statement for the General Store Café is as follows: "To host our customers in a welcoming, eclectic, and wholly unique environment while attentively serving top-notch food created with local, healthy, and natural ingredients. To be a part of our community fabric by providing a setting ripe with local art, music, food, and hospitality—all in an environmentally conscious atmosphere."

Product Sustainability Plan

What are the initiatives and efforts under way now and new initiatives being started? What will be the benefits to the Café? (See Table 7.7.)

Organic fruits and vegetables
Organic free range meats
Local free range eggs
Vegan and vegetarian dishes
Compostable carryout containers
Filtered water system for cooking and cleaning
Rain barrel water collection
On-site herb garden
Local food vendors and suppliers
Our own handcrafted recipes
Live, local music weekly
Local arts, gifts, and collectibles
Local organic free trade coffee
Fresh fruit smoothie bar
GSC catering available
Banquet facilities for parties and meetings
Large screen television and video
500 sf stage
Local non-profit fundraisers monthly
Commitment to green building space
Grab-n-go deli for your convenience
Strong environmental commitment
Local board of directors and investors

Marketing and Transparency Plan

The expansion project of the General Store Café has made it possible to begin a variety of sustainability initiatives that are currently under way, including rain catchment, energy reduction, wastewater reuse and reduction, etc. In order to attract more customers, the marketing

Table 7.9   Transparency Plan

Sustainability Initiative	Data Source / Certifications	Transparency Strategy
Local Sourcing		
Energy Reduction		
Energy Diversification		
Water Reduction		
Community Support		
ROI to Investors	Provide an opportunity for local patrons to become part of the investment community	Provide an opportunity for local patrons to become part of the investment community

plan shown in Table 7.8 outlines the messages and delivery modes to share information about the benefits of the Café and its efforts toward becoming more sustainable.

Transparency Plan (Certifications)

What certifications will be completed (if any), and what will be the level of transparency of the Café's sustainability initiatives? (See Table 7.9.)

Your sustainability strategic plan becomes a working document that drives the business toward greater levels of greenth from year to year. The main consideration is to what degree the company is meeting its financial goals while expanding its sustainability initiatives. Ideally, the financial interests and sustainability interests are united and merged as part of the overall business plan.

A key difference between this strategic plan and others is this plan's emphasis on documenting and measuring outcomes from quarter to quarter and year to year for the business and for the community.

It's important to see the extended footprint beyond the confines of the building and the business itself as well as all the relationships around the enterprise. When customers begin to see the relationships they contribute to a business through increased transparency of the company's changing footprint, their awareness potentially will have the effect of increasing demands on other businesses, not just a restaurant like the General Store Café.

This effect of pushing the limits of the corporate footprint beyond the walls of the building to the greater community is discussed in the next chapter.

8

Smart Green Leadership

The economy is a wholly owned subsidiary
of the environment.

—*Timothy Worth*

Dialogue is properly a gift relationship as well.
When we speak together in a dialogue,
we are speaking in a way that seeks to
contribute one to the other.

—*William Isaacs,* Dialogue and the Art of
Thinking Together

A CRISIS IS A TERRIBLE THING TO WASTE

Just when it seemed to be safe to venture outside again—secure venture capital, get a loan, reinvest in a new product line—despite high gas prices, a weakening economy, and inflationary prices, banks had to declare bankruptcy and the market had to crash harder than ever since the Great Depression. Every location on the planet has been affected. Can such turbulent times still provide a glimmer of hope for entrepreneurs to continue their enthusiastic bid for sustainable enterprises?

Every one of the business leaders I spoke with indicated hope for the future and, in fact, a belief that the global financial crisis provides a silver—or green—lining. Even though the encroaching climate changes are threatening our way of life, the recent economic crisis helps to clarify further the need to change approaches and try new ways to conduct business: The U.S. presidential election brought more clearly into focus the need for energy independence through alternative fuel sources as much as through drilling for oil and gas close to home; the upsurge in the youthful voting block also indicates a shift toward more sustainable solutions; and the downfall of so many financial institutions with many ancillary companies and industries due to corporate greed and a regulatory blind eye forces us to reflect on the need for integrity from corporate leaders.

For the rank-and-file business owner and corporate manager, the economic crisis is a source of pain as everyone recalibrates their lifestyles and reorders their lives to ride out the storm. Meanwhile, there is an opportunity to rethink products and services: How are they made? How are they shipped? How far do they come? Do my suppliers share the same values for sustainability that I have? Who else can I obtain products and services from? It's a unique time to reassess everything not only to find significant cost savings but also to reach an increasing number of new customers desiring to become more sustainable as well.

My own father built the second phase of his business out of the ashes of a fire that destroyed his retail shoe store. He would not have made the necessary changes in his business model without experiencing a total loss in his retail business. Many entrepreneurs, including myself, experience failure in the form of business loss or tragedy, only to re-create themselves with a renewed vision. Even in the face of an economic slowdown, tougher loan requirements, and fewer venture capital dollars, intrepid entrepreneurs and forward-thinking managers find the necessary vision and strategy to navigate the rough waters.

A local restaurant set out an idea bowl for its customers, and every month a new question was posted for patrons to fill out responses to. Results from these questions were printed for everyone to view the following week. One question asked was: "What is your most important life lesson?" An 84-year-old gentleman responded: "Never, ever, ever, ever, ever, ever give up." I could feel some of the regret in his message but understand it perfectly. Whatever life throws at you, remember this message.

Smart Green companies are keenly aware of this message, and when crisis occurs the opportunity for change can become that much clearer. They rely more heavily on their willingness to take risks; fulfill a dream in spite of the odds; build an organization based on integrity and respect for their employees, the community, and the environment; and carefully measure their results for cost savings and return on investment.

With a consumer base increasingly sickened by the excesses of financial institutions, investment banks, and corporations generally seeking a quick return without regard to longer-term implications, such as the mortgage-lending debacle and the auto industry missing the fuel-efficiency window of opportunity, consumers will increasingly be more attracted to companies with a clearly defined sustainability mission. So each company should reflect: "What's a company like yours doing in a fine crisis like this?"

NOT IN MY BACKYARD

The pain of the economic downturn will likely worsen and persist for months or years. Not every company will survive it, even Smart

Green companies. The best outcome is for those leaders who navigate through the crisis with wisdom, frugality as needed, and innovation. Meanwhile, while the economy is thrashing the global community, global warming has not taken a holiday. Major changes in carbon emissions, reduction in the use of fossil fuels, and better stewardship of oceans, forests, and freshwater still need to be made. Some analysts believe we are on a short leash of just three to four years before we reach the point of no return for major shifts in our climate, oceans, and air. Others believe we have a decade or so.

As the climate change threat persists, other issues and challenges have emerged as organizations strive to define sustainability for themselves and begin implementing new initiatives to challenge the status quo. It's natural to remain blissfully unaware of the implications of the changes occurring in our environment and to see our companies as insignificant in the larger picture. Or we may even decide that it's somebody else's problem, much like the musical chairs game of shifting our waste from one location to another until it falls into the region of least resistance—usually that of the poor and disenfranchised. The mantra of "not in my backyard" is alive and well. Each of the examples of challenges that follow illustrates the complexity and the importance of increased dialogue and proactive development of strategies to overcome them.

Diversity of Definitions

Since there is no definitive answer to "What is sustainability?" accepted as a standard, the subject is in process. In every industry, there will be a spectrum of definitions, approaches, and measured outcomes for sustainable initiatives that will not seem like enough effort for some and like unapproachable effort for others.

Fred Abousleman, executive director of the National Association of Regional Councils, doesn't define sustainability "as an environmental issue, but rather a holistic economic development issue."

For Cliff Tweedale, executive director of Headwaters Regional Development Commission in Bemidji, Minnesota, making the case for sustainability in the "real world" among traditional business leaders is the greatest challenge: "If I go to our local food co-op, the term *sustainable* makes a project a great idea, but with the more traditional leaders that term is a challenge and maybe has a negative response. I think that the traditional community is becoming more open to the ideas, and they are actually more accepting than I originally thought they would be."

"We are really at the early stage. The greatest obstacle we need to overcome is: 'Can you find a way to make it work in the market?' It is also a challenge working with the local government. When we ask them, 'What do you think?' they say, 'Yeah, it's a great idea.' But when we ask, 'What do you think about supporting this project with a dollar commitment?' they are not as willing to support us. Doing the right thing is still more expensive. That may not be the case for long, but it is now."

The challenge is deciding for yourself what the definition of sustainability is for you and how you can be implementing your strategy to maintain and grow your business successfully. Smart Green companies gain insights from their customer base, which is likely to be more profitable than comparisons with their competition or companies from other industries.

Split Resources

At a recent sustainability conference for higher education, many of the exciting ideas and innovations for greening universities were overshadowed by one very important issue: split resources.

Often capital projects that universities undertake are funded from a variety of sources, and planning for these improvements takes place sometimes years before implementation. Many of these financial resources are suddenly being split between converting or building new facilities that are LEED certified, which can cost hundreds of thousands or even millions of dollars, in lieu of possibly more pressing needs such as long-overdue renovations of 50-year-old historic buildings on campus. With the pressure of attracting more students interested in sustainability, there is a rush to spend on green planning to keep up with the demand. The decision to split the resources between sustainability initiatives and long-standing needs in other facilities, as well as direct education costs such as salaries, benefits, and new faculty, needs to be carefully managed to meet the overall goals of the institution, not just short-term marketing targets.

Like universities, Smart Green companies must also decide on priorities based on their missions, values, markets, and budgets to establish the right value for the right time, not just a "feel good/do good" project at the expense of other more appropriate projects that benefit the company.

Cultural Differences

Let's face it—most participants in the sustainability arena are white, an inadvertent inheritance from the environmental activism days. Global warming affects everyone, so there is no one group, nationality, race, or culture that owns the issue, and cultural diversity to improve the dialogue and inspire more innovation is a necessity for lasting change.

Business tends to be the great equalizer, and there are many minority-owned businesses in the United States. Competition will inspire entrepreneurs of any stripe to adapt to sustainable methods if the customer is applying the pressure. Cultural diversity goes beyond just hearing different voices and perspectives. It is also a critical component of social justice to be meaningfully reflected upon—and necessary for the prevention of environmental and economic decisions made at the expense of minorities.

Smart Green companies value the contribution and participation of a variety of cultures in the discovery of sustainability initiatives within their community, which has the proven cumulative effect of improving their business.

Certifications

The proliferation of certifications across every industry may create not only overlap of green validation but possible confusion about what is really sustainable. Certifications can be categorized into three basic groups: regulation, which is a stamp of approval from a government agency or accredited institution to validate compliance with government regulations; proprietary certification, which is provided by an independent organization with a set of standards defined by the sponsoring organization; and single-attribute certification, which certifies standards for a specific outcome such as energy or air quality.

Certifications can be helpful in providing a shorthand validation for an organization's sustainability efforts. They can be very expensive and time-consuming, however, especially when there are numerous certifications within one industry. Smart Green companies decipher the marketplace carefully for the benefits of one certification over another, scrutinize the standards themselves to ensure authenticity and true benefit to the triple bottom line, and calibrate their budgets and resources available to ensure the best return on investment while avoiding greenwashing.

Transparency

One of the greatest challenges facing companies desiring to become more sustainable is revealing their troublesome carbon footprint, energy consumption, or toxic waste dumping. Even if the company is making progress, any disclosure of actual pollutants output, poor air quality, water use, fuel use, and so on becomes the target of criticism. For the next few years, transparency will be a process of managed perception until there is a balance in the maturity of the company and marketplace to accept changes and intent to change as companies transition to sustainable models of reporting.

At a recent conference called the Green Media Show, Mike Connor of HOW Online[1] reports from one session presented by Robert Pojasek, an internationally recognized expert on business sustainability, that "Transparency and accountability are the two key words in measuring business performance related to environmental issues and that sustainability should be about doing more of a good thing, not just doing less of a bad thing." Smart Green companies seek to increase the level of transparency as they determine it to meet their strategic goals and further increase transparency as the market rewards them.

Funding

Can companies claiming to be sustainable use this attribute to attract loans, venture capital, or angel investment? There is no question that going green is hot and on the rise in the investment community. Silicon Valley is reportedly shifting its attention toward the trillion-dollar energy market by investing in alternative energy companies. Tax breaks, matching funds from foundations, and government grants may help to supplement some investment capital and loans, but the level of investment is extremely high to meet the energy requirement for the U.S. alone—thousands of times more capital invested than during the dot-com era.

Creative means to fund sustainability projects are being developed in all sectors, especially in higher education where "two sophomores at Macalester College draw on their experience creating a revolving loan fund as follows: The high initial cost of many sustainability projects can often deter campuses from implementing them, despite the fact that such projects often have long-term cost savings. A revolving loan fund helps overcome this challenge by providing zero or low interest loans to fund money-saving sustainability projects. A portion of the savings generated from these projects is then reinvested into the fund until the loan has been paid off."[2]

The challenge remains to make innovative products with a proven marketplace and strong revenue model, especially in the tight financial markets prevailing after the October 2008 crash.

Global Standards

Not everyone agrees that climate change is real, nor does everyone agree that it's man-made. With this level of skepticism still rampant, it is no wonder that it's so difficult to inspire global action to avert a climatic catastrophe. The challenge is to translate the effects of what's known scientifically about air and water quality and temperature change due to the greenhouse effect into collective action for stopping current polluting behavior, and to begin reversing the damage. If one country takes steps toward sustainable change and others do not, the goal will never be achieved.

According to Simon Gordek, CEO of AccountAbility, the need for improved global standards and the process of creating them has never been greater: "Global markets are really an amalgam of interlinked national and regional markets, framed by legislation passed by national governments, sometimes informed by international agreements covering everything from postal standards to trade tariffs to labor and environmental standards. The rules are, in short, a mess, built up over decades by thousands of different public and private organizations. Furthermore, many of our ways of developing international standards are in disrepair and disarray. . . . Yet standards are hugely important in ensuring that companies behave responsibly in ways consistent with sustainable development. Whether it be about corruption, climate change, or privacy rights on the Internet, we cannot rely alone on the responsibility of individual companies or the seduction of business gains to ensure that business does the right thing."

Smart Green companies seek to stretch their own footprint to their partners and suppliers, and extend the change up to the point of extraction and down to waste after consumption. Global standards are needed to guide all humanity to a common vision and plan of action.

Turf Wars

As the popularity of sustainability increases, so do the organizations and businesses that claim to own the definition, territory, and domain in which they reside. A regional representative in Little Rock, Arkansas, mentioned that turf battles are his greatest challenge: "When you have organizations that are in competition with each other, there can be some opposition and a reluctance to work together. It is hard for some businesspeople to move out of the mind-set of competition into one of collaboration."

Public, private, and governmental organizations promoting sustainability are trying to garner many of the same constituents in every industry. The challenge is to permit the various groups to coexist and, it is hoped, provide unique contributions to an extremely broad field. Many of these organizations can join together in public/private partnerships, for example, to leverage their networks and resources for the greater benefit to the community.

Change Models

Incremental change versus pendulum shift will be a constant challenge between individuals and organizations for many years to come. Depending on the assumption that climate change will reach a no-return tipping point in a few years or that all business is bad if its model is unlimited growth helps to perpetuate the belief that change must be swift and significant. If the assumption is that the effects of climate change can be averted through collective effort and maintained globally as the status quo, then incremental change with business enterprise leading the innovations and managed growth will be the model of choice.

Business Value

In the rush and enthusiasm to implement sustainable practices, the low-hanging fruit of cost savings is usually plucked without consideration for the longer-term stability of establishing actual business value. Consumers may be attracted to the particular certification you achieved, the donation made to a charity, or the B100 fuel you use for your diesel trucks; but at the end of the day, your products and services must produce a profit. Determining business value tends to be more elusive because the benefit is difficult to determine, unlike determining savings on your budget.

Performance metrics and isolating business impact through a process of intervention and control where you try an initiative in one location and not another for comparison may be necessary to ensure actual return on investment. Smart Green companies thrive when business value is determined to be significant by stakeholders such as investors, banks, and consumers. These issues and challenges in the discovery and implementation of sustainability will continue to persist and many others will arise, because anything of value demands a struggle.

Lyle Estill, founder of Piedmont Biofuels, expresses his commitment to the cause of sustainability and why he stays committed: "Probably because we have an abiding dissatisfaction with the way the world works. If you were to ask the average guys from our company, they would say that things in the world are not okay: war, global climate change. . . . We are very interested in the knowable and the doable. There are 38 people on the project and every one of them has a sense of that. Eating a strawberry from Chile versus eating a local one is a very different choice. There are all types of external factors in terms of labor, energy consumption, environmental damage that are often not taken into consideration by the consumer.

Sustainability is at the heart of our mission. We are trying to build a business that can last and be sustainable. The alternative of not taking advantage of current crises in the global economy coupled with the worsening climate changes is too great to ignore."

In spite of the tightening money availability, it is hoped that great leaders, ideas, and companies will still thrive, attract investment, and grow. Estill explains that it's their passion for the model that motivates him and his employees to stay in business: "We did not jump into this because of money. We are motivated by other means. We exist by means of creative finance: family, friends, employees, passionate mission-driven folks who are willing to get paid below-market salaries and put their money and efforts into a different concept of business. This whole notion that 'I'm going to make a whole bunch of money and then give back'—it doesn't work. More business as usual under the green banner is what got us into this mess—not what is going to get us out."

The issues and challenges with sustainability strategies are daunting, but they are the necessary part of all of our businesses. As I mentioned before, all businesses are on the spectrum of sustainability; it's just some that don't realize it and will potentially be negatively impacted by inaction. I often face challenges in my own business that seem to come all at once, sometimes down and sometimes up. On the downside I may be pinched for cash flow, bills are piling up, customers are requiring more hand-holding, there are lower than expected quarterly sales, and—oh, yes—a global economic collapse. As an entrepreneur, I have learned to use a variety of methods to keep my focus during the hardest of times and have found that others use similar methods:

First, periodically reaffirm your beliefs and your mission. Sometimes the pressure of deadlines, personnel issues, and growth or downturns make us see the trees and not the forest. Recalling and reflecting on why I'm in business in the first place and what I'm trying to accomplish helps to minimize the impact of the daily pressures. I had told myself that these pressures would come and that I would always remember the bigger picture in the long term.

Second, count your blessings. This is not a religious act, though it could be if you want. I reflect on all of the benefits and joys I've had as an entrepreneur and the progress I've made from humble beginnings. I look at the skills, experience, and travels I have done to make my life and the lives of my family, friends, colleagues, and clients more enriching. Without acknowledging these blessings, none of the work and struggles would be worth it.

Third, analyze where you are in relation to your expected time lines. The wheels of change and growth often turn slowly, and if you had planned well in the beginning you would have realized that at various points in the cycle, growth can be less and pressures can be greater. Reminding yourself of your current position and where you need to go helps to relieve some of the worry and stress.

Fourth, connect with your mentors. I always have a short list of colleagues and mentors whom I trust to give me insight and encouragement in the critical moments when I need it. Don't be afraid to tap into these critical assets in your life.

Fifth, decide what will it take for you to quit. It's usually the sum total of life's pressures that gets us down and may push us over the edge to end our dream and lifework. If taken as individual issues, each pressure is actually small and insignificant in comparison to what we want to accomplish. One script I use with myself: "Is this what's going to make you quit your dream?" I often will work harder and smarter when I see each problem as a less significant obstacle.

BUILDING SMART GREEN COMMUNITIES

Like individuals and organizations, communities can evolve toward a sustainable practice through a process of change as long as there are opportunities for strong leadership in communicating a common vision and a goal to be achieved. Reaching across socioeconomic lines, small and large businesses, public/private partnerships, cultural and racial diversity, advocacy groups for the environment and social change, youth groups, higher education, and so on all contributes to enriching the community's economic, social, and environmental health.

The power of the Internet to facilitate the development of local, regional, national, and global social networks of like-minded individuals and organizations is increasingly being harnessed for sustainability initiatives. Social networking sites, green online encyclopedias, and sustainable business directories are all serving to link customers with vendors and vice versa. Learning best practices and calling companies on greenwashing can occur at much more rapid rate.

Moreover, the normal barriers between people are breaking down. Where before there may have been distrust and animosity, it's possible to share a common goal that is mutually beneficial to the entire region. The path of development toward becoming a Smart Green community is no different than that of an individual or a company. For many communities, the tipping point has already occurred and they are ready to embark on trying something new.

GreenBiz.com's latest annual release of "the state of green business" showed that companies' marketing is way out in front of the actual outcomes. Katy Ansardi, executive director of Sustainable North Carolina is similarly cautious about the trend in business toward sustainable practices: "A lot of companies are on board, but many more are curious and trying to figure out what is going on. The main change we have noticed over the last 3 years is the increased awareness of sustainability by the business community. There has been a sea change in terms of credibility and the number of organizations implementing sustainability initiatives. However, there is still much skepticism and 'greenwashing' because it is so hard to say what is or isn't sustainable. The fundamental rules of the game of business haven't changed—there is still an overarching pressure for short-term returns to the shareholders that trumps everything else. A fundamental shift in strategic thinking is needed that looks at issues in more holistic manner and responds to the rapidly changing, complex global conditions we face today. Business leaders need to be talking about how to make this change more acceptable because peer references are so important. Business managers will respect the viewpoint of someone who has walked in their shoes before that of academia, nonprofits, or government. They also need a support infrastructure that allows them to quantify these new risks and opportunities and to talk about them in the language of business. There is a tremendous need for new analytical tools, strategic frameworks, and connectivity with peers and mentors."

For Aaron Nelson of the Chapel Hill–Carrboro Chamber of Commerce, "I'm a father with a five-year-old and a two-year-old, and that has given me real perspective about the importance of the future. Like me, business owners and managers are realizing the importance of paying attention to issues of climate change. Every day I see businesses reaching a tipping point as they come to terms with their personal and business-centered reasons to 'do the right thing' for the community and the environment. They just need to know how and to have access to good information.

"Recently, the customer is providing more push toward going green and sustainable, and the business owners are feeling a pull toward making change as they realize the importance of making and their ability to make a difference. Business leaders and I realize there is an interdependency among a community's social needs and challenges, environmental stewardship, and a successful economy. If one suffers, the others likely suffer as well. I'm committed to learning how to create a balanced, thriving, sustainable community." Aaron represents many business leaders from a regional perspective inspired by the upsurge of interest in trying to lead along a new path.

Likewise, regional planners are merging their insights and experience with the demands and vision of sustainability not just for individual companies, institutions, and cities, but for entire regions that may span several cities and in some cases several states as a mega-region. In fact, at a recent conference for the Alliance for Regional Stewardship (ARS), a national, peer-to-peer network of regional leaders working across boundaries to solve tough community problems, the theme was "innovate" and the topics were centered around sustainability. Members attended from the business, government, education, and civic sectors and shared a common commitment to collaborative action and achieving results.

Fred Abousleman, executive director of the National Association of Regional Councils, which works with local and regional government agencies to provide advocacy, training, and information, clarified that "Sustainability is not a term we use much. We look at it not so much as an environmental issue, but rather a holistic economic development issue. Every opportunity involves business interests as we work to collaborate with local governments and businesses to help them move forward together rather than competing for resources. For successful communities to thrive, they need to partner with businesses; and for businesses to be successful, they need to be an integral part of the community. Where we build a project or program we aim to help governments work better together, to reach more people, and to save money. We are successful when partners see the regional issue and express a desire to share the cost and rewards of a regional development project."

Dennis Andrews, president and CEO of the Richmond-Wayne County Chamber of Commerce in Richmond, Indiana, reported that the organization "recently adopted a new comprehensive plan document with a sustainability emphasis. For us, sustainability has yet to be fully defined and operationalized into our approach to development in a comprehensive way. Our Economic Development Corporation recently decided to plan to develop a Green Park in the northwest part of the county. There is a growing awareness of our need to be good stewards of the environment as we aggressively strive to compete in the global marketplace. We mentioned our sustainability focus during a recent visit to Japan to attract investment. I think there also is the feeling that this is, at the very least, a trend that is well received generally, provided it does not translate into significantly higher development costs."

Regional planners may inadvertently or by proxy reinforce sustainable initiatives in a region even if they are not part of a mission or operating plan. For example, Frank Beal, executive director of Chicago Metropolis, which focuses on creating collaborations with other organizations and is developing a new kind of "civic entrepreneurship" in the region, is very clear about making the Chicago metropolitan area a better place to live and work in. Without an explicit definition of sustainability for the organization, "the things we promote and advocate are transportation policy that reduce congestion and VMT [vehicle miles traveled]—we see transportation as a cost of doing business, not because of carbon footprint or emissions. We support a more integrated community in terms of housing types and more jobs, not for any social equity reasons, but having to do with the high cost of segregated communities and the high cost of transportation. We support a much more progressive criminal justice system because the current system is way too expensive and there is not enough crime prevention. We support early childhood education because the payoff to economic development is enormously high, with every dollar invested bringing $7 payback to the community."

Cliff Tweedale, executive director of the Headwaters Regional Development Commission, similarly does not have a specific mission for sustainability but realizes that affordable housing is critical for the five-county region around the Bemidji, Minnesota, community to succeed economically. "With our housing development projects we have created different tools for affordable housing development, including a purchase/rehab model as opposed to doing new construction. We recognize a need to change densities in order to make housing more affordable, and we respond through a rethinking of design and construction values to incorporate green features that are cost effective.

"Right now doing sustainable, green housing is more expensive, but we have broadened our projects based on being open to sustainable products and services. In the long term, we will have projects that encompass the sustainability or green values without stating that. Right now, projects are framed as sustainable development or green projects. As it becomes imbedded in the core values of the community, we will bring those values to the general projects. We will be thinking about a good housing project, not a sustainable project."

Some regions are experiencing an upsurge of interest from a variety of sectors to see their regions thrive in the context of sustainable practices. One regional planner defines sustainability as the improvement of quality of life among its citizens. "We are in the process of a countywide economic development strategic planning process with a diverse steering committee that consists of several dozen people from different socioeconomic backgrounds, nonprofits, business communities, education leaders, and faith-based organizations. The majority of our members consistently attend our meetings, which indicates commitment and interest.

"We want to change a no-growth area to a growth area. Without bringing people together to create an understanding, to be a part of the process, and to buy into the solutions, we won't be very effective at creating change. We held a community input survey online and focus groups in which 1,500 people participated. I, and the organization facilitating the surveys, believe that is an extremely strong number and it proves that the community is wanting this type of process and leadership to emerge."

THE NEW CURRENCY

Theories and approaches for sustainable strategies and green marketing plans aside, three things drive an entrepreneur to take the plunge and start a company despite all the risks that doing so entails: a vision compelling enough to start something new and maintain it through the ups and downs; talented individuals to discover new innovations and deliver quality products and services; and financial means to get the engine started and to keep it going through all of the organization's stages of growth. Without vision, the company flounders; without talented people, there is no creative breakthrough; and without capital, the company perishes.

Recently, more has been added to this recipe the fundamental belief that conducting business, and indeed living our own personal lives, is more fulfilling and meaningful, better for business, and better for the planet when we begin to *care* about it. During this rapid shift toward sustainable innovations, truly innovative companies will experience their success not only because of creative breakthroughs of new technologies and fuel sources or great marketing plans, but even more in the *way* they do business—the degree to which participants feel a sense of purpose in their work—which won't show up on any balance sheet.

This new currency, caring and purpose, is imperceptible to traditional means of reporting because it is an attribute of visionary leaders, corporate stakeholders, employees, and customers realizing that they are an integral part of an interdependent larger system. Each is rewarded for supporting the other. This economic/environmental/social system is becoming increasingly sensitive to the attitudes and behaviors of every person on the planet. From the wheat farmer in Swaziland to the CEO of a major airline, how each contributes to the whole and their feelings of purpose and contribution are fast becoming a necessity to overcome barriers to a sustainable world.

Population growth, limited resources, political unrest, and an increase in demand for living the Western way of life are pushing humanity to the brink of disaster on all fronts. Realizing our interdependence and responsibility to each other and each aspect of these systems is what it means to care—a critical success factor for any business to survive and thrive in the era of sustainability. This new connection with each other and new ways to express the new currency of caring is beginning to show up at an emerging phenomenon: sustainability forums. At a recent regional forum in partnership with the United States Chamber of Commerce and its nonprofit affiliate, the Business Civic Leadership Center, participants from a diverse group of businesses and organizations shared insights that struck me as different from other business gatherings I had attended before.

The quality of the questions and the concerns expressed reflected a genuine interest in how each person and organization could make a difference for the community and for the environment. Even the issue of not enough racial diversity being represented in the gathering was expressed as a concern that everyone shared to ensure that in the planning for future gatherings, racial and cultural dimensions will be considered in order to attract more diversity. Participants were able to contribute their own perspectives about what sustainability means to them, which covered the spectrum of the levels of greenth, as well as various stages of change, they were at personally and in their organizations. This created a sense of solidarity around a common theme beyond business networking and announcements of charitable giving. Large and small businesses, civic organizations, social change organizations, and environmental groups not only have a new *currency of caring* to learn about and act upon, but they also have a new language emerging that unites them toward a common purpose that has tangible benefits for each participant.

This new currency and lexicon of sustainability is opening doors of community building not only between businesses and consumers but also between previously contentious organizations such as social change groups and businesses, businesses and environmental groups, social change groups typically in competition for funds with environmental groups, and each of these organizations with local, state, and government agencies. Though there is still plenty of distrust between groups, the common concerns, language, opportunities, and aware-ness of urgency bring everyone together to discuss possibilities and to formulate positive change strategies.

THE LEADERSHIP ROLE

Many business leaders from a variety of sectors are rising up and taking a stand for sustainable practices not only in their own organizations but also in their communities. They are utilizing their skills in organiza-tional development, entrepreneurial spirit, and leadership abilities with a goal toward sustainability to lead to a significant effect in personal and community change. "Sustainability, beyond being a widely thrown net of practices and operations that contribute to a more sustainable planet, is in and of itself a way to reach out beyond ourselves, and beyond a single group," said Barb Eichberger, founder of the LinkedIn Sustainability Working Group. "It is a way to a future of practices that increase our awareness, to stay more greatly connected with who we are in this planetary community and how we can contribute most to positive ends within that reality in everything we do."

For Eric Friedenwald-Fishman, president and creative director of the Metropolitan Group, the leadership mantle has been enhanced by the recent changes in the marketplace: We are seeing a "radically more aware public of the sustainability issues." When he started years ago, clients where not asking for sustainability. "Today, if you are not working to improve the environment and social equity, you are potentially out of business." Eric realized that the changes in public awareness from the public were also occurring within his own organi-zation. As in many organizations, many of the principles of sustain-ability were already present, but were just unnamed values: "There is a deep personal passion among members of staff and management. Sustainability is intrinsic to our mission where we craft strategic and creative products for nonprofits and businesses that have a positive impact on the environment and/or social equity of our communities. It makes excellent economic sense."

Eric also speaks about the long-term commitment that sustain-ability leadership requires: "It's never over. There are new things we can do each year, such as ensuring all of our new offices are on the train line to the airport, adaptive reuse of historic buildings, and advocacy about light fixtures with building owners, while recognizing that new opportunities will present themselves in the future."

Responsiveness of businesses to sustainability values may come easily for many companies, and especially for those leaders in the nonprofit community when it comes to the elements of social equity and the environment. But what about everyone else struggling to make ends meet? How does the leadership role for sustainability factor in business success, longevity, and making a real impact on people and communities? In short, what are the attributes required of the new kind of leader emerging in the age of sustainability?

Successfully running your own company or managing a large department where you have responsibilities—raising money and managing a budget; setting goals; creating a strategy and implementing it; communicating with staff, stakeholders, and clients; and keeping a vision alive—requires a special kind of person. My belief is that this form of leadership is part nature and part nurture. You have to already have some of the skills built into your personality, but you also have to work very hard, gain knowledge and skills, learn from others, and fail and fail again. It's common to hear from many successful leaders from all kinds of organizations that initial failure in their endeavors was part of the learning process.

Overcoming self-doubt actually is the greatest battle—the one between your ears. There are as many books and theories about leadership as there are successful leaders. As helpful and insightful as these books are, each of us is capable of establishing a short list of critical success factors for effective leadership. From my own experience of starting and running companies, seven attributes of what makes a leader successful have emerged:

1. *Effective leaders have a strong sense of self.* Some call it a thick skin, but leaders are able to take criticism and attacks of their ideas on one side and handle praise and glory in both the best and the worst of times. Also, the internal dialogue of a leader is about honestly checking your motives and actions regularly as well as affirming that failure, though not a good option, is often an opportunity to learn or a new door opening.

2. *Effective leaders are ongoing learners.* No one can claim to know everything that is needed for every situation; however, there is a skill required of a leader to be open to many possibilities, look for trends, listen to mentors, and learn what's necessary for every contingency.

3. *Effective leaders are skilled communicators.* Leaders are always part of a group requiring a great deal of communication. Inspiring others, articulating a plan, solving problems, resolving conflicts, and keeping silent at the right time are all necessary skills for leaders. All forms of communication are used, including written and spoken language, body language, eye contact, physical contact, emotional expression, and cultural understanding.

4. *Effective leaders empower others to complete their tasks.* Most people strive to become good at what they do and contribute an important part of the overall project or enterprise. Leaders are skilled in empowering others to see their roles and purposes not only in completing the basics but in striving for completion of what they started and excellence in everything they do.

5. *Effective leaders see a project through to the end.* In developing software, there is an 80/20 rule that implies that 80 percent of a project is the easy part, whereas it's meeting the deadlines and excellence in the last 20 percent that is the difficult part. Leaders must be both visionary and action-oriented. They have to be able to look around corners, anticipate delays, compensate for budget shortfalls, and still meet deadlines and complete what they have started.

6. *Effective leaders create and maintain a vision.* Whether at the start-up phase, during implementation, or in long-term growth, leaders see the beginning, middle, and end with the ability to mitigate risks while keeping a vision in front of the organization. Though the vision may change, the fact that a leader is always able to articulate and inspire others to achieve it marks their level of success.

7. *Effective leaders have a deep-rooted sense of purpose.* In addition to a vision, there is also conviction. Something more than a great

idea is motivating a leader to strive against seemingly impossible odds, create something from nothing, and persevere over years of adversity: meaning and purpose. Without meaning and purpose, leaders would not be able to inspire others to the levels of hard work and investment required to accomplish their goals.

There are obviously many other attributes of successful leaders, and in many ways everyone is a leader of their own lives. The purpose of highlighting these seven attributes is that they can be applied directly to being successful in your sustainability strategic planning process. The differences between Smart Green leaders and greenwashing leaders are striking, as illustrated in Table 8.1.

Smart Green companies are led by individuals and teams who are constantly aware of and developing their leadership skills. For example, as you prepare to develop a sustainability strategy by becoming aware of the issues in your community and the environment, the attributes of being an ongoing learner, having a strong

Table 8.1

Smart Green Leader	Greenwashing Leader
Aware of social, environmental, and economic indicators of their community.	Aware of the specific indicators for their industry and their customers.
Planning for sustainability based on ability to implement and maintain.	Planning based on immediate competitive advantage.
Seeks insights from mentors and sector experts as well as from the non-profit, policy, and government sector.	Seeks insights from trade periodicals, sector experts, and internal teams only.
Measures success on profit and the expanded footprint of company, employees, products, manufacturing, delivery, extraction, and waste.	Measures success from profit and the company footprint only.

sense of self, seeing the trends before they are completely manifested by your consumers, and being able to envision a new future for your company are necessary. As you begin to define sustainability in relation to your personal life, your business practices, your business goals, and the mission for your company, you will be called upon to articulate and inspire others to invest capital, lend you money, work for you, complete projects, and buy your products and services.

You must discover your level of greenth and adapt your ability to start and maintain your implementation plan for sustainability in a realistic, authentic way. In the planning and implementation phase, a lot of trial and error will occur since there is no recipe for success in going green other than making sure you have planned according to your ability to implement and sustain your initiatives and that you are acting on what you know and believe more than for financial gain alone. Measure the business impact to ensure that the value of your initiatives is balanced among the various impacts of the triple bottom line. Smart Green leaders are analysts of their own processes, seeing themselves in the third person, and use business intelligence as much as their intuition to guide their way. As your company matures and grows, your level of greenth is likely to grow as well, which may spur a major shift in your vision—re-creating your company again with the intent to become more fully sustainable. Not everyone is going to see it and follow you, but you must trust that the timeliness, company values, community, and environment will gain from your decision.

Through each of these stages of the planning process, it's extremely important to foster a wide and intentional connection with others striving toward the same goals, including other businesses, nonprofits, policy groups, and government agencies. Keep widening the circle of your footprint. Move beyond the borders of your personal actions, those of your employees, and those of your organization to clients, suppliers, and manufacturers, as well as services for delivery, extraction, and waste. Over time, the impact of every decision you make not only will potentially attract new customers, but will impact all of the business relationships, supply chains, employees, investors, and professional services to link with you in like mind. You become a leader not only of ideas but, through commerce, a leader by example. Multiplied by thousands of other small businesses, the negative impacts on the environment will diminish tremendously, and the tangible benefits realized by the community at large will increase commensurately.

Similarly, the flexibility of an entrepreneurial enterprise, in contrast to a nonprofit entity, is evident in how the goals of each type of organization are achieved. For the commercial enterprise, sustainability has the implication of making money while also having a positive impact on people and planet. For the nonprofit, the goal is implementing a project to solve a problem with a limited budget in a limited time with no requirement for profit; the nonprofit seeks financial sustainability through additional funding.

One example is a situation I encountered when I traveled to Uganda to deliver computer-based learning systems in rural areas. A small hospital with 20 health-care practitioners couldn't benefit from Internet access because the line stopped at the nearby church just outside of the village. Our systems would not work without access to the Internet, so we called the Internet service provider (ISP). The nonprofit organization providing training didn't include an Internet budget for installation and ongoing costs, so a request for Internet access had never been placed. Since there was no request for access from the hospital, the ISP didn't offer service. As entrepreneurs, we met with the ISP representatives and struck a deal with them to offer Internet access if they would pay for installation. Our company paid for the first year's access until the hospital could take over the cost in the following year's budget. We also suggested linking the line from the church to the hospital to save money. From the nonprofit's perspective, it couldn't be done. From the entrepreneurial perspective, it was a hurdle that had to be overcome to keep our business growing.

Changes in leadership toward a Smart Green model are perceptibly increasing. As organizations begin incorporating sustainability principles into their mission statements, human relations policy manuals, marketing plans, and sales pitches, leaders soon realize that deeper awareness of the environment and their community is required. This means leaders and teams are by necessity becoming more reflective of their roles, their decisions, their metrics and outcomes, and how they communicate their value more accurately and meaningfully.

In any economic climate, but especially in a down economy, the need to demonstrate business value is intrinsic to a company striving to become more sustainable. Reliance on analytical data becomes more of an imperative than reliance on anecdotal data. Another significant change is the concept of the leader being a servant and steward. Though not a new concept, leaders deciding to implement their vision of a sustainable organization have to realize their role as a servant to the community and a steward of the environment. The leader who is also a servant has the qualities of being able to see through the eyes of employees, investors, customers, partners, and suppliers, as well as increasing his or her perception of the needs of the community. As the leader progresses through levels of change in terms being able to take action and derive insight and meaning from perceiving the company through the eyes of each of these stakeholders, the leader is able to increase the role as a servant in meeting the needs of each in relation to the goals of the organization. The servant/leader is able to speak more effectively, communicate the vision, and be able to fine-tune the marketing messages and products and services to the needs of each stakeholder.

The measurable gains from this role are many: There is better retention of employees, as they perceive their interests are being heard and served; the investor believes the investment is being utilized for the best rate of return while also working for the good of social and environmental impact; suppliers and partners are more likely to work with this leader more efficiently and to be willing to make changes as necessary to accommodate changes in level of greenth as the leader changes; customers receive a better product and price with more insights into their needs and wants; the greater community benefits both directly and indirectly from the example the leader establishes in the company's extended footprint; and the company will possibly attract higher-quality employees and new customers.

Likewise, the environmental steward leadership role is based on the degree to which the leader is aware of and understands the impacts and benefits of decisions related to environmental issues such as water, energy, air, land, and waste. As the leader becomes increasingly bio-aware and energy-aware, every decision is based on known impacts on the environment. This awareness enables leaders to be more transparent and demonstrate to their own stakeholders as well as to the general public the changes in impact over time that they may be having on energy efficiency, reduction in water consumption from public sources or groundwater, increased conservation, decreased CO_2 emissions, better use of waste, and increased levels of greenth among their supply chain partners from year to year. Once a leader has begun to incorporate the means of thriving financially, becoming more of a servant/leader and an environmental steward, he or she now has the basis for building a truly sustainable enterprise—a Smart Green company that can begin not only to innovate new technologies that benefit the planet but to pioneer a new way of doing business.

LEADERSHIP FOR INNOVATION

Every day in the news a small-town entrepreneur announces a breakthrough in green technology. From converting a Prius to a battery-powered-only vehicle to creating a fuel source for cars from water; from earthworm dung for fertilizer to more efficient solar cell technology; from wind farm installations to a chicken dung methane gas collection facility; from biofuels powering airplanes to sandals that you don't throw away (you chop them up as compost)—innovations are springing up in every sector. With the increase in available venture funds and an open and increasing customer interest, the sky is the limit for the entrepreneurial community to respond. Many innovations will be born in Orville and Wilbur Wright fashion in a garage or bike shop, while others will be discovered in university research labs or corporate facilities. The key factor to consider is that with the momentum building, largely prompted by the high cost of energy and increased consumer demand, the ability to build, market, and maintain new green products on one level needs to be in balance with the ability to lead, market, and sustain the organization with emphasis on outcomes of the triple bottom line. For the crisis generated by climate change to be overcome, we have to consider significant changes in behavior as consumers and business owners. Green products need to be built by Smart Green companies—those that are active in discovering the meaning of sustainability for themselves, for their communities, and for the environment.

Leadership for innovations in sustainability will be represented by a large spectrum of companies throughout every sector. Most of the innovations will be initially made in technology, such as new sources of energy, engineering new processes, and chemical compounds that are harmless or less dangerous to human health and to the environment from the point of extraction through to their waste. In addition to these innovations, there will be a new kind of company emerging: a Smart Green company that prides itself not only on discovering new technologies for energy efficiency or a new type of car but on its relationships with other companies, its employees, the community, and the environment. These companies will behave with higher moral and ethical standards and still thrive financially. In the near future, it will be because of the transparency of their products and practices that they will be increasingly successful.

Appendix

SMART GREEN AWARENESS RESOURCES

Climate Change/Global Warming

- United Nations Environment Programme, "Climate Change" (www.unep.org/Themes/climatechange/).

- United States Environmental Protection Agency (USEPA), "Climate Change" (www.epa.gov/climatechange/).

- *Abrupt Climate Change: Inevitable Surprises*, from the National Research Council (Washington, DC: National Academy Press, 2002).

- *The Change in the Weather: People, Weather, and the Science of Climate*, by William K. Stevens (New York: Bantam Books, 2001).

- Wikipedia, "Ecological Footprint" (http://en.wikipedia.org/wiki/Ecological_footprint).

"The phrase 'climate change' is growing in preferred use to 'global warming' because it helps convey that there are changes in addition to rising temperatures."—The National Academies (quote from the USEPA Web site)

Energy

- United States Department of Energy (www.doe.gov/energysources/index.htm).

- United States Energy Information Administration (www.eia.doe.gov/).

- Energy Matters (http://library.thinkquest.org/20331/types/).

- Wikipedia, "Renewable Energy" (http://en.wikipedia.org/wiki/Renewable_energy).

- *Sustainability and Environmental Impact of Renewable Energy Sources*, edited by R. E. Hester and Roy M. Harrison (Cambridge, UK: Royal Society of Chemistry, 2003).

- *The Post-Petroleum Survival Guide and Cookbook*, by Albert Bates (Gabriola Island, Canada: New Society Publishers, 2006).

- *Winning Our Energy Independence*, by S. David Freeman (Layton, UT: Gibbs Smith, 2007).

Sustainability

- United States Environmental Protection Agency (USEPA), "Sustainability" (www.epa.gov/Sustainability/).

- Wikipedia, "Sustainability" (http://en.wikipedia.org/wiki/Sustainability).

- Global Footprint Network (www.footprintnetwork.org/index.php).

- *Blessed Unrest: How the Largest Social Movement in History Is Restoring Grace, Justice, and Beauty to the World*, by Paul Hawken (New York: Viking, 2007).

- *The Ecological Footprint: Accounting for a Small Planet*, film narrated by Dr. Mathis Wackernagel.

- *The 11th Hour*, documentary film produced and narrated by Leonardo DiCaprio et al.

- SustainAbility, consulting firm with a very informative Web site, including case studies (www.sustainability.com/).

Going Green

- *Animal, Vegetable, Miracle*, by Barbara Kingsolver (New York: HarperCollins, 2007).

- *Small Is Possible: Life in a Local Economy*, by Lyle Estill (Gabriola Island, Canada: New Society Publishers, 2008).

- *Plan B 3.0: Mobilizing to Save Civilization*, 3rd ed., by Lester R. Brown (New York: W.W. Norton, 2008).

- *Living Green*, by Greg Horn (Topanga, CA: Freedom Press, 2006).

- *Radical Simplicity*, by Jim Merkel (Gabriola Island, Canada: New Society Publishers, 2003).

- *Simple Prosperity*, by David Wann (New York: St. Martin's Griffin, 2007).

- Planet Green (http://planetgreen.discovery.com/).

- Green Options (http://greenoptions.com/).

Bio-Aware

- *Annual rainfall:* How Stuff Works, annual rainfall map for the United States (http://maps.howstuffworks.com/united-states-annual-rainfall-map.htm).

- *Waterways:* International Rivers (www.internationalrivers.org/); American Rivers (www.americanrivers.org/site/PageServer); National Oceanic and Atmospheric Administration (NOAA)'s National Weather Service, "Water" (www.weather.gov/ahps/).

- *Land forms:* United States Geological Survey (USGS), "Geology" (http://geology.usgs.gov/index.htm).

- *Weather patterns:* NOAA's National Weather Service, "Graphical Forecasts" (www.weather.gov/forecasts/graphical/sectors/).

- *Flora and fauna:* National Wildlife Federation (www.nwf.org/wildlife/); World Wildlife Fund (www.worldwildlife.org/); State Wildlife Resources Commission/Agency.

- *Agricultural zone:* United States Department of Agriculture (www.usda.gov/wps/portal/usdahome); United States National Arboretum, USDA Plant Hardiness Zone Map (www.usna.usda.gov/Hardzone/).

- *Air quality:* NOAA's National Weather Service, "Air Quality" (www.weather.gov/aq/).

- *Groundwater tables:* United States Geological Survey (USGS), "Groundwater Information" (http://water.usgs.gov/ogw/).

- *Change initiatives:* Green Map System (www.greenmap.org/); Global Climate Change Research Explorer (www.exploratorium. edu/climate/biosphere/index.html); Climate Prosperity Project (www.climateprosperity.com/).

Socially Aware

- *Cultural diversity:* Global Alliance for Cultural Diversity (http:// portal.unesco.org/culture/en/ev.php-URL_ID=24468&URL_ DO=DO_TOPIC&URL_SECTION=201.html); American Life (http://amlife.america.gov/); FedStats (www.fedstats.gov/qf/).

- *Literacy rates:* Wikipedia, "Countries by Literacy Rate" (http:// en.wikipedia.org/wiki/List_of_countries_by_literacy_rate).

- *Changes in income over time:* United States Census Bureau, "Income" (www.census.gov/hhes/www/income/income.html).

- *Crime rates:* Sperling's BestPlaces, "Crime Rate Comparisons" (www.bestplaces.net/crime/).

- *Birth and death rates:* United States Census, "Population Finder" (http://factfinder.census.gov/servlet/SAFFPopulation?_ submenuId=population_0&_sse=on).

- *Employment:* United States Bureau of Labor Statistics (www.bls .gov/).

- *Economic growth:* United States White House, "Jobs and Economic Growth" (www.whitehouse.gov/infocus/economy/); United States Chamber of Commerce (www.uschamber .com/default).

- *Support organizations:* ePodunk, "Community Demographics" (www.epodunk.com/demographics/index.html); Idealist.org (www .idealist.org/).

- *Change initiatives:* Open City Foundation (www.opencityfound .org/en/index.asp?lan=en); Center for the New American Dream (www.newdream.org/).

Energy-Aware

- *Sources:* United States Department of Energy (www.doe.gov/energysources/index.htm); *Sustainable Energy: Choosing among Options*, by Jefferson W. Tester, Elisabeth M. Drake, and Michael J. Driscoll (Cambridge, MA: MIT Press, 2005).

- *Uses:* Wikipedia, Energy Conservation (http://en.wikipedia .org/wiki/Energy_conservation).

- *Impacts on air, land, water, human health, ecology, economy:* Low Impact Living (www.lowimpactliving.com/); United States Environmental Protection Agency (USEPA), "How Does Electricity Affect the Environment?" (www.epa.gov/cleanrgy/energy-and-you/affect/index.html).

- *Improving diversity of sources:* United States Department of Energy, "Energy Efficiency and Renewable Energy" (www.eere .energy.gov/); *Earth: The Sequel—The Race to Reinvent Energy and Stop Global Warming*, by Fred Krupp and Miriam Horn (New York: W.W. Norton, 2008).

- *Incentives for change:* Database of State Incentives for Renewables and Efficiency (www.dsireusa.org/); Tax Incentives Assistance Project (www.energytaxincentives.org/).

- *New technologies:* Wikipedia, "Energy Development" (http://en .wikipedia.org/wiki/Energy_development); Industrial Technology Research Institute, New Energy Technology Division (www.netd .itri.org.tw/).

Regionally Aware

- *Changes in population:* United States Census Bureau, "State and County QuickFacts" (http://quickfacts.census.gov/qfd/).

- *Transportation:* Association of Metropolitan Planning Organizations (AMPO), MPO directory (www.ampo.org/directory/index.php); United States Department of Transportation (www .dot.gov/).

- *Energy:* United States Department of Energy, regional energy profiles (www.eia.doe.gov/emeu/reps/).

- *Water:* United States Geological Survey (USGS), local offices for water resources (http://water.usgs.gov/local_offices.html).

- *Land:* Nature Conservancy (www.nature.org/); United States Department of Agriculture, Natural Resources Conservation Service (www.nrcs.usda.gov/); United States House of Representatives, Committee on Natural Resources (http://resourcescommittee.house.gov/).

- *Urban sprawl:* Wikipedia, "Urban Sprawl" (http://en.wikipedia.org/wiki/Urban_sprawl); Sprawl Watch Clearinghouse (www.sprawlwatch.org/).

- *Pollution:* Wikipedia, "Pollution" (http://en.wikipedia.org/wiki/Pollution); Scorecard, The Pollution Information Site (www.scorecard.org/).

- *Employment:* United States Bureau of Labor Statistics (www.bls.gov/); United States Equal Employment Opportunity Commission (www.eeoc.gov/index.html).

- *Health:* National Center for Health Statistics (www.cdc.gov/nchs/); World Health Organization Statistical Information System (www.who.int/whosis/en/).

SMART GREEN NETWORKING RESOURCES

The mission of *Co-op America* (www.coopamerica.org/) is to harness economic power—the strength of consumers, investors, and businesses—to create a socially just and environmentally sustainable society. It publishes the *National Green Pages*, provides the Business Seal of Approval for those businesses successfully completing its screening process and determined to be socially and environmentally responsible, hosts the annual Green Business Conference and several Green Festivals, produces a newsletter, and offers other business and consumer networking and educational opportunities.

SustainableBusiness.com (www.sustainablebusiness.com/) provides global news and networking services to help green businesses grow, covering the following sectors: renewable energy, green building, sustainable investing, and organics. The Web site provides a good source for news, investment opportunities and advice, a job listing service, requests for business connections, an events calendar, and a resource list.

The *Sustainable Business Institute (SBI)* (www.sustainablebusiness .org/) was founded in 1995 to provide companies committed to sustainability a venue for sharing best practices and promoting shared goals. Its mission is to motivate private enterprise to initiate, institutionalize, and communicate sustainable business practices, thereby increasing profitability and shareholder value. SBI awards its Seal of Sustainability to honor businesses and business leaders throughout the world that have distinguished themselves through the implementation of sustainable business practices that rise above the norm. The site includes an events calendar, a program list, and an invitation to participate in one of SBI's user groups.

The *Business Alliance for Local Living Economies (BALLE)* (www .livingeconomies.org/) is an international alliance of independently operated local business networks dedicated to building local living economies. Its mission is to catalyze, strengthen, and connect networks of locally owned independent businesses. The Alliance envisions a global economy made up of linked local economies, comprised of businesses that are local, green, and fair. It is the world's fastest-growing network of sustainable businesses. Since 2001, it has helped spawn close to 60 BALLE networks representing more than 15,000 entrepreneurs across the United States and Canada. The Alliance provides tools and resources for small business leaders to learn how to be more sustainable.

The *International Business Leaders Forum* (www.iblf.org/) works with businesses, governments, and civil society to enhance the contribution that companies can make to sustainable development. The Web site offers publications of research aimed at different industries, five key programs that tackle development issues, relevant news stories, case studies, an events calendar, and advice on embracing transition to a sustainable business model.

The *World Business Council for Sustainable Development (WBCSD)* (www.wbcsd.org/) is a CEO-led, global association of some 200 companies dealing exclusively with business and sustainable development. The Council provides a platform for companies to explore sustainable development; to share knowledge, experiences, and best practices; and to advocate business positions on these issues in a variety of forums, working with governments, as well as nongovernmental and intergovernmental organizations. Members are drawn from more than 35 countries and 20 major industrial sectors. The Council also benefits from a global network of about 55 national and regional business councils and regional partners.

Business and Sustainable Development (www.bsdglobal.com) is a site developed by the International Institute for Sustainable Development (IISD) (www.iisd.org/). The site explains the strategies and tools that companies can draw on to translate an aspiration of sustainability into practical, effective solutions. Case studies from around the world are provided as an example of each measure. The site covers current issues, strategies and tools, markets, banking and investment, working with nongovernmental organizations (NGOs), and training opportunities.

For additional information about how to effectively implement sustainable strategies in your business or organization, as well as stay up-to-date with case studies, new tools and resources, and relevant sustainability news go to MySmartGreenBusiness.com.

Notes

Chapter One   The Green Rush

1. *An Inconvenient Truth* (Paramount Classics and Participant Productions, 2005).
2. "The Next Industrial Revolution: William McDonough, Michael Braungart and the Birth of the Sustainable Economy" (Earthome Productions, 2001).
3. David Suzuki and Holly Dressel, *Good News for a Change: How Everyday People Are Helping the Planet* (Vancouver, Canada: Greystone Books, 2003).
4. R. K. Pachauri and A. Reisinger, eds., *Climate Change 2007: Synthesis Report: Contribution of Working Groups I, II, and III to the Fourth Assessment Report of the Intergovernmental Panel on Climate Change* (Geneva, Switzerland: IPCC, 2007), 104.
5. Nicholas Stern, "The Economics of Climate Change," *The Stern Review, Cabinet Office—HM Treasury*, January 2007.
6. Andres Edwards, *The Sustainability Revolution* (Gabriola Island, Canada: New Society Publishers, 2005).
7. John Elkington, *Cannibals with Forks: The Triple Bottom Line of 21st Century Business* (Oxford, UK: Capstone Publishing Ltd., 1999).
8. Amory Lovins, L. Hunter Lovins, and Paul Hawkins' seminal book, *Natural Capitalism* (New York: Back Bay Books, 2000).
9. Fred Krupp and Miriam Horn, *Earth: The Sequel—The Race to Reinvent Energy and Stop Global Warming* (New York: W. W. Norton, 2008).
10. Fred Krupp, "The Motherload," *Fast Company*, April 2008.
11. Joel Makower, Ron Pernick, and Clint Wilder, "Clean Energy Trends," *Clean Edge*, March 2008. http://cleanedge.com/reports/ (downloaded pdf on May 16, 2008).
12. Selection from Ron Pernick, "Cafe Musings (or How Clean Tech Is Becoming Ubiquitous)," *Clean Edge, The Clean Tech Market Authority*. http://cleanedge.com/views/index.php?id=5328.
13. National Technology Readiness Survey (NTRS) report, 2007, by Rockbridge Associates, Inc., 10130 G Colvin Run Road, Great Falls, VA.

14. David Ehrlich, Cleantech Group, "Accelerating the Next Wave of Innovation," Cleantech Network, LLC, March 24, 2008. http://media.cleantech.com/2620/consumer-cleantech-market-could-hit-104b (accessed May 27, 2008).

15. "Getting from Green to Gold: Retail Success Factors and Outcomes," The Aberdeen Group, July 2008.

16. Jennifer Kaplan, "Six Retail Trends You Need to Know About," *Ecopreneurist*, August 20, 2008.

17. "Study: CEOs Battle to Keep Up with the Pace of Change," IBM, May 9, 2008; Lifestyles of Health and Sustainability (LOHAS). www.lohas.com/articles/101282.html (accessed May 18, 2008).

18. Selection from Ron Pernick, "Cafe Musings (or How Clean Tech Is Becoming Ubiquitous)," *Clean Edge, The Clean Tech Market Authority*. http://cleanedge.com/views/index.php?id=5328.

Chapter Two   Taking the First Step—Becoming Aware

1. Kathryn Kobe, "The Small Business Share of GDP, 1998–2004," Economic Consulting Services, LLC, Washington, D.C. 20036. Under contract SBAHQ-05-M-0413 [37] pages.

2. U.S. Small Business Administration, Office of Advocacy, March 2001.

3. Mark Horowitz, "Two Environmentalists Anger Their Brethren," *Wired*, September 25, 2007.

4. Adapted from J. O. Prochaska, C. C. DeClemente, and J. C. Norcross, "In Search of How People Change: Applications to Addictive Behaviors," *American Psychologist* 47 (September 1992): 1102–1114.

Chapter Three   Defining a Smart Green Company

1. William McDonough and Michael Braungart, *Cradle to Cradle: Remaking the Way We Make Things* (New York: North Point Press, 2002).

2. David Suzuki and Holly Dressel, *Good News for a Change: How Everyday People Are Helping the Planet* (Vancouver, Canada: Greystone Books, 2003).

3. *Apollo 13*, Universal Studios, 1995.

Chapter Four   Smart Green Strategic Planning
1. Kerry Napuk, *The Strategy-Led Business* (New York: McGraw-Hill, 1996).

Chapter Five   Measuring Sustainability Outcomes
1. Scott Leibs, "Sustainability Reporting: Earth in the Balance Sheet," *CFO*, December 1, 2007.
2. Thomas H. Davenport and Jeanne G. Harris, *Competing on Analytics: The New Science of Winning* (New York: McGraw-Hill Ryerson Agency, 2007).
3. Foundation for Sustainable Community.

Chapter Six   Marketing Green and Transparency
1. Dick Wolfe, "Red-Hot for Green Businesses," *ecoAmerica*, November 1, 2007.
2. Dennis Walsh, "Beyond the Green Wash: The Competitive Advantage of Green Marketing," *ManageSmarter.com*, July 17, 2008.
3. Accenture, "End-Consumer Survey on Climate Change," 2007.
4. Dennis Walsh, "Beyond the Green Wash: The Competitive Advantage of Green Marketing," *ManageSmarter.com*, July 17, 2008.
5. "Who Are the Green Consumers?" *BSDglobal.com*, 2007. www.bsdglobal.org/markets/green_who.asp.
6. Nathan Adkisson, "Responsibility Rules," *ManageSmarter.com*, July 15, 2008.
7. Jonathan Tannenbaum, "Will Green Marketing Bring You the Green?" *ManageSmarter.com*, July 8, 2008.
8. TerraChoice Environmental Marketing, "The Six Sins of Greenwashing." www.terrachoice.com/files/6_sins.pdf.
9. "Who Are the Green Consumers?" *BSDglobal.com*, 2007. www.bsdglobal.org/markets/green_who.asp.

Chapter Eight   Smart Green Challenges and Leadership
1. HOW online, www.howsmatter.com.
2. Association for the Advancement of Sustainability in Higher Education press release, November 13, 2008.

Index

Aaron Nelson, 164
Aberdeen Group, 16
Abousleman, Fred, 154, 164
Accenture, 116
accountability, 157
AccountAbility, 158
action stage, 30
adaptation, 75–77
adult literacy, 21
Advanced Energy, 52, 117
advertising vs. public relations, 126
affordable housing, 139
Africa, 9, 45
Alliance for Regional Stewardship
    (ARS), 25, 164
alliances, 25
alternate fuel sources, 152
analysis and reflection, 87–88
analysis of current state, 84–86
analytics approach, 97, 100–102
analytics-based metrics vs.
    assumptions-based metrics, 101
analytics importance, 108–109
Andrews, Dennis, 165
An Inconvenient Truth (Gore), 3
Ansardi, Katy, 163
Aquaeras, 69
Arkansas, 33, 159
assessment styles, 101
assumptions-based metrics vs.
    analytics-based metrics, 101

balanced scorecard process, 102
banking, 28

Barnett, Roger, 83–84
BB & T Corporation, 28
Beal, Frank, 165
Beasley, Bill, 117
Beijing Olympics, 114
beliefs and assumptions, 63
beliefs and mission, 161
benchmarking, 110
BetterWorld Telecom, 40
bio-awareness, 35–36
biofuels, 133–134
blessings, 161–162
bloggers, 123–124
blogs, 125
BMG Marketing, 125
brain plasticity, 77–78
Braungart, Michael, 44
Brundtland Report, 42
BSDglobal.com, 118, 127
budgeting, 135
builders, 27–28
Builders of Hope, 52, 139
building smart green communities,
    162–167
Burt's Bees, 3
business case study, 104–108
Business Civic Leadership
    Center, 168
business relationship analysis, 60–61
business relationships, 89
business value, 159–162
    creation or destruction, 133–134
    defined, 133
    demonstration, 132–133

measurement metrics, 135–137
perception management,
    137–140
business value measurement, 95–98

C40 Large Cities Climate
    Leadership Group, 50
California, 11, 127
Canada, 127
*Cannibals with Forks: The Triple
    Bottom Line of 21st Century
    Business* (Elkington), 7
carbon footprint, 51, 52, 121, 157
cash flow analysis, 61–62
categories for the strategic planning
    framework, 88–90
CEO transitions, 132
certifications, 156–157
    Cradle to Cradle, 54
    Green Seal, 54, 127
    Leadership in Energy and
        Environmental Design (LEED),
        54, 82, 85
    proprietary certification, 157
    Scientific Certification Systems, 127
    single-attribute certification, 157
    transparency plan (certifications),
        148–149
CFO magazine, 97
Chandler, Michael, 27–28
Chandler Design-Build, 27–28
change
    awareness of the need for, 81–82
    fear of, 81
    five stages of, 30–31
change models, 159–160
Chapel Hill-Carrboro Chamber of
    Commerce, 164
Chapel Hill Chamber of Commerce,
    25–26
Chicago Metropolis, 165

China, 12
Clean Edge, 15
climate change, 5–6, 7
"Climate Change 2007" (IPCC), 5
Climate Change 2007 (survey), 116
Clinton Climate Initiative, 50
Clorox, 3
coffee economy, 76
commercial enterprise, 174
Common Ground Green Building
    Center, 29
communities of committed
    individuals, 37
company biosphere analysis, 141
Connor, Mike, 157
consumer choice, 119
consumer education, 120
consumer trends, 122
contemplation stage, 30
corn production and use, 43
corporate biosphere, 57–62
    business relationship analysis,
        60–61
    cash flow analysis, 61–62
    footprint analysis, 58–59
    product life cycle analysis, 59–60
corporate financial goals vs. value
    creation, 134–135
cosmetic tasks, 136
cost-benefit analysis, 110–111
costs and benefits of progressive
    thought, 165–166
cost savings, 38–40
Cradle to Cradle (McDonough and
    Braungart), 44, 57
Cradle to Cradle certification, 54
cultural diversity, 156
cumulative environmental
    impact, 72
currency of caring, 168
current state analysis, 84–86

dashboards, 96, 97, 108
David Suzuki, 48
Diggit, 125
disclosure of sustainable activities, 50
Doerr, John, 14

Earth Day, 13
earth-friendly terms, 123
Earth: The Sequel (Krupp), 44
*Earth: The Sequel-The Race to
    Reinvent Energy and Stop Global
    Warming* (Horn and Krupp), 12
eco-entrepreneurs, 27
economic benchmarks, 110
economic crisis as opportunity,
    152–153
economic growth, 11
"Eco Pulse", 120
eco terms, 123
education, 34–35
effective leadership factors, 170
effective marketing, 115
Eichberger, Barb, 37, 169
80/20 rule, 172
Einstein, Alfred, 46
Elkington, John, 7
employee hiring and sustainability,
    138
employee satisfaction and
    sustainability, 138
energy awareness, 36
energy independence, 152
Energy Star, 28, 85
entrepreneurial enterprise vs.
    nonprofit emphasis, 174
entrepreneurial spirit, 21–23
entrepreneurial spirit, attributes
    of, 22
entrepreneurs, 11
entrepreneurship and sustainability,
    24–26

environmental attitudes, 126
environmental benchmarks, 110
Environmental Choice program, 127
environmental footprints,
    69–75
environmental stewardship,
    43–44
Estill, Lyle, 20, 160–161
Estill, Mark, 20, 116
ethanol, 43
exploitation, 162

Facebook, 120–121, 125
facilities budget, 136
facilities managers, 132
failure
    as change agenda, 153
    as learning process, 170
fair-trade (term), 3
Fisher, Eileen, 119
footprint analysis, 58–59
Footprint magazine, 33
footprints, 69–75
Ford, Henry, 44–46
forests, 25
Foundation for Sustainable
    Community, 26
Friedenwald-Fishman, Eric, 169
funding, 157–158

General Motors, 94
General Store Café, 20, 25, 60
General Store Café smart green
    profile, 140–150
    company biosphere analysis, 141
    description, 140–141
    greenth level analysis, 141
    marketing and transparency
        plan, 148
    product sustainability plan,
        147–148

sustainability mission statement,
    141–143, 146–147
transparency plan (certifications),
    148–149
"Global CEO Study" (IBM), 17
Global Reporting Initiative (GRI),
    109, 128–129
    for transparency, 56
global standards, 158–159
global warming debate, 2–3
gold rush to green rush, 10–12
Good News for a Change (Suzuki and
    Dressel), 4, 48
good vs. less bad, 74–77, 157
Gordek, Simon, 158
Gore, Al, 3
green awareness, 35
GreenBiz.com, 163
green bubble, 13
Green Business Review, 119
green consumer, 116–124
green fatigue, 13, 119
Green Home Council, 117
green investing, 14–15
Green Media Show, 157
green product prices, 47
green rush, 24, 38, 120
    evidence of, 12–13
    gold rush to, 10–12
    momentum of, 32
Green Seal certification, 54, 127
green terms, 123
"greenth" development
    levels of, 53–57
    level 1 (basic recycling and green
        practices), 54–55
    level 2 (internal resources
        including human resources),
        55–56
    level 3 (production to distribution
        redesign), 56

level 4 (sustainable practices at
    highest current levels),
    56–57
greenth level, personal, 173
greenth level analysis, 141
green vocabulary, 3
greenwashing, 40
    defined, 123
    vs. Smart Green, 49–53
    vs. sustainability, 42
gross domestic product (GDP), 21

Hall, Amy, 119
Hartford, Bob, 95
Hartman Group, 121
Hawkins, Paul, 12
Haw River Festival events, 25
Headwaters Regional Development
    Commission, 154, 166
Holly, Dressel, 48
homebuilding industry, 116
Horn, Miriam, 12
HOW Online, 157, 193
Huntley, Blakley, 28

IBM, 17
Illinois, 50
immigrant workers, 139
implications recognition, 82–84
increasing business value awareness,
    99–100
India, 12
Indiana, 165
innovation, creativity, growth, and
    meaning, 88
International Energy Alliance, 14
Internet, 123, 162
Internet access, 174
intervention, 106–107
inventions, 10–11
ISO 14000, 128

Johanson, Richard, 81–82

Kenefick, James F., 40
Krupp, Fred, 12, 44

landscaping companies, 80, 139
leaders as servant and steward, 175
leadership attributes, 172
leadership for innovation,
    176–177
Leadership in Energy and
    Environmental Design (LEED)
    certification, 54
leadership role, 169–176
LEED certification, 82, 85
less bad vs. good, 74–77
LinkedIn social network, 37, 125
LinkedIn Sustainability Working
    Group, 169
Literacy South, 22
litigation for change, 24
Living Local (Estill, L.), 20
locally grown, shade-grown (term), 3
locavores, 76
Loving, L. Hunter, 12
Lovins, Amory, 12

maintenance stage, 30
Makower, Joel, 119
Manchester College, 158
marketing and transparency
    plan, 148
marketing green and transparency,
    114–129
  green consumer, 116–124
  niche market to mainstream,
    116–118
  red-hot green, 114–116
  smart green marketing plan
    development, 124–129
McDonough, William, 28–29, 44, 74

measurement plan, 94
measuring sustainability outcomes,
    94–111
  analytics approach, 100–102
  analytics importance, 108–109
  benchmarking, 110
  business value measurement,
    95–98
  cost-benefit analysis, 110–111
  increasing business value aware-
    ness, 99–100
  metrics selection, 102–103
  moon shot, 94–95
  return on investment (ROI)
    analysis, 110–111
  savings on investment and return
    on investment, 98–99
  Smart Green business case,
    103–108
  sustainability metrics, 109
mentors, 22, 38, 52, 81, 83, 162
metrics, 106
metrics selection, 102–103
Metropolitan Group, 169
Mexico, 139
Minnesota, 154
mission statement, 62–66
moon shot, 94–95
Mosaic, 22
M-Squared Builders, 35
Murray, Nancy, 52, 139
Myers, Michele, 35, 36
MySpace, 125

Napuk, Kerry, 68–69
National Association of Regional
    Councils, 154, 164
Natural Capitalism (Lovins, A., L.
    Lovins and Hawkins), 12
natural terms, 123
NBC, 114

Nelson, Aaron, 26
Nery, Paulo, 33
Netherlands, the, 128
networking, 36–37
network marketing, 83–84
new currency, 167–169
new environmentalism, 15–18
niche effectiveness, 114
niche market to mainstream,
    116–118
Nigeria, 45
no GMO (genetically modified
    organism) (term), 3
nonprofit emphasis vs.
    entrepreneurial enterprise, 174
non-toxic homes, 83–84
North Carolina, 20, 25, 27, 29, 35,
    52, 81–82, 117, 122, 133–134,
    139
not in my backyard, 153–162
    business value, 159–162
    certifications, 156–157
    change models, 159–160
    cultural diversity, 156
    funding, 157–158
    global standards, 158–159
    split resources, 155–156
    transparency, 157
    turf wars, 159–160

Obama, Barack, 9
objective tools, 102
Ocean, Danny, 8–9
oil crisis of 1970's, 12
oil development and production, 45
oil prices, 9
Old Heritage Builders, 27, 117
O' Mara, James, 139
Oregon, 25, 52
organic (term), 3
organic farming, 85

organic food, 121
outcomes and impacts, 87–88

participants, 106
peer-to-peer references, 163
perfect storm, 9–10
performance and profitability,
    46–49
Pernick, Ron, 15
philanthropy, 48
Piedmont Biofuels Industrial LLC,
    20, 116, 160
planning and implementing
    strategy, 86–87
planting trees, 43–44
plasticity, 77–79
Plaxo, 125
Pojasek, Robert, 157
PracticalEco, 33
pre-action stage, 29
pre-contemplation stage, 30
preservation and conservation
    alliances, 25
product definition, 17
product life cycle, 89
product life cycle analysis, 59–60
product sustainability plan, 147–148
profitability and performance,
    46–49
proprietary certification, 157
Proventia Solutions, 94
public and private alliances, 10, 126
public relations vs. advertising, 126

RainEscape, 33, 69
rainforest-friendly (term), 3
Ray, Chad, 27, 117
recycled materials demand, 46–47
red-hot green, 114–116
reflection, 34
regional awareness, 36

regulation, 156
relationships, 73
Relay for Life events, 25
Remick, Vance, 20, 25, 60
research, 126
return on investment (ROI), 4, 22,
    49, 90, 96
  analysis of, 110–111
  measurement of, 102
  metrics for, 100
  vs. savings on investment, 94
revolving loan fund, 158
Richmond-Wayne County Chamber
    of Commerce, 165
roofing materials, 17
Rouse, Bill, 34

savings on investment (SOI)
    approach, 98
savings on investment and return
    on investment, 98–99
savings on investment vs. return on
    investment, 94
Scientific Certification Systems, 127
sector-based ecosystem, 73
shade-grown, (term), 3
Shaklee, Forrest C., 83–84
Shaklee Corporation, 83–84
share axiom, 115
Shelton Group, 119
Sierra Club, 25
Silicon Valley, 158
Silverwood Bingham Ridge, 95
single-attribute certification, 157
smart green, 13
smart green business case
  executive summary, 104
  introduction and overview, 105
  assumptions and methods,
      105–106
  intervention, 106–107

metrics, 106
participants, 106
results and conclusions, 108
smart green challenges and
    leadership, 152–177
  building smart green communi-
      ties, 162–167
  economic crisis as opportunity,
      152–153
  leadership for innovation,
      176–177
  leadership role, 169–176
  new currency, 167–169
  not in my backyard, 153–162
smart green companies
  becoming, 140
  defined, 32–33
smart green companies building,
    131–149
  becoming a smart green com-
      pany, 140
  business value creation or
      destruction, 133–134
  business value demonstration,
      132–133
  business value measurement
      metrics?, 135–137
  business value perception manage-
      ment, 137–140
  corporate financial goals vs. value
      creation, 134–135
  General Store Café smart green
      profile, 140–150
smart green growth
  analysis and reflection on out-
      comes and impacts, 87–88
  analysis of current state, 84–86
  awareness of the need for change,
      81–82
  innovation, creativity, growth, and
      meaning, 88

planning and implementing strategy, 86–87
recognition of implications, 82–84
seven tiers of, 80–88
systems view approach, 86
smart green marketing plan development, 124–129
smart green vs. greenwashing, 49–53
social awareness, 36
social benchmarks, 110
social equity, 25, 44–46
social justice, 156
socially responsible investors (SRI), 109
social networking, 37, 58, 61
social networks, 120, 125
Solar Solutions, 122, 139
split resources, 155–156
stakeholders, 64–66, 88–89
statistical analysis tools, 95
Stern, Nicholas, 6
Stock Building Supply, 34–35
Strategic Measures, Inc., 132
strategic planning and sustainability, 68–69
strategic planning models, 91
strategic road map, 90–91
strategic spending, 135
strategy, planning and implementing, 86–87
Strategy-Led Business (Napuk), 68
sustainability
    definitions of, 27, 42–43, 154–155, 166
    and employee hiring, 138
    and entrepreneurship, 24–26
    vs. greenwashing, 42
    lure of, 26–32
    meaning of, 6–8

and strategic planning, 68–69
    whole systems approach to, 51
sustainability (term), 3
sustainability initiative, 136
sustainability leadership crisis, 169–170
sustainability marketing research firm, 121
sustainability metrics, 109
sustainability mission statement, 141–143, 146–147
sustainability outcomes, 89
Sustainability Reporting Guidelines, 128
"Sustainability Working Group", 37
sustainable activities disclosure, 50
Sustainable North Carolina, 163
sustainable strategy
    adaptation, 75–77
    plasticity, 77–79
systems view approach, 86
System Vision Program, 52

Tannenbaum, Jonathan, 120
10 percent rule, 135
The Institute for Sustainable Development, 58
"The Next Industrial Revolution" (Lovins, A., L. Lovins Hawkins), 3–4, 7
The Stern Review, 6
Toma, Paul, 29, 95
toxin-free (term), 3
transparency, 56, 126–127, 157
Trevathan, Zemo, 132
Triangle Multiple Listing Service, 28
Triangle PolySteel, 28–29, 51
triple bottom-line, 6, 42, 52, 53, 64, 95, 96, 157
turf wars, 159–160

Tweedale, Cliff, 154, 166
Twitter, 125

Uganda, 174
United Nations Intergovernmental
    Panel on Climate Change
    (IPCC) Fourth Assessment
    Report, 5
United States Chamber of
    Commerce, 168
universities, 155–156
University of North Carolina at
    Chapel Hill, 81–82
U.S. National Technology Readiness
    Survey (NTRS), 16
U.S. Patent Office, 11
Utah, 52

Valtonen, Mikko, 94, 97
VanZeeland, Tom, 33, 69

Volunteers in Service to America
    (VISTA), 21

Wal-Mart, 25
Webinars, 126
Werbach, Adam, 25
Westbrook, Elena, 40
Westergaard, Ann, 83–84
Western way of life, 168
whole systems approach to
    sustainability, 51
"Will Green Marketing Bring
    You the Green?"
    (Tannenbaum), 120
World Wide Web, 22

Yoder, Bradley, 28–29, 51
YouTube video blogs, 126

Zely and Ritz (restaurant), 122